Amy S. Mitchell

Daily Whispers

Inspirational Affirmations

to Unleash Your
Inner Power and
Radiance

Contents

Introduction

I welcome you to the World of Affirmations, Beautiful and Wonderful Woman. I'm glad you're here, and as a woman myself, I hope you'll find some useful tools here to help you build your confidence and discover the strength and awesomeness that is within you. You may sometimes forget or even doubt it, but believe me, the power to create the life you want is right within you. And all magic starts with a thought.

You may already know that the greats of this world emphasize the role of thoughts in shaping one's life. Our thoughts and beliefs influence our behavior and, in turn, our experiences and outcomes. This means that when we think positively and believe in ourselves and our abilities, we are more likely to take actions that lead to success. On the other hand, when we think negatively and doubt ourselves, we are more likely to avoid challenges and difficulties. Great people from all walks of life, such as scientists, athletes, business people and artists, emphasize the role of positive thinking in attracting success and happiness.

And that is where affirmations come in.

They are a powerful tool that, when used properly, can help you heal, achieve your goals, and improve your quality of life. It's a technique that allows us to focus on the positive aspects of life rather than the problems and difficulties.

That's why in this book you will find carefully selected affirmations for us women to help you in various areas of life such as self-esteem, health, finances, success, love and many others. Each affirmation has been specially prepared to help you achieve a specific goal and increase your positive thinking.

Importantly, I don't mean simply repeating these affirmations in your head. I want you to write down them to increase their impact on your psyche and subconscious. The written word is one of the most powerful ways to reinforce positive beliefs in our subconscious.

But that's not all. You'll also find tips on how to create your own affirmations, allowing you to individualize your affirmation practice and tailor it to your needs and goals.

Whether you are just starting out or are experienced in affirmation practice, this book is for you. Start using affirmations now and see the positive impact they have on your life.

"I am a woman with thoughts and questions and shit to say. I say if I'm beautiful. I say if I'm strong. You will not determine my story—I will."

— Amy Schumer

"We need to reshape our own perception of how we view ourselves. We have to step up as women and take the lead."

— Beyoncé

"Be a first rate version of yourself, not a second rate version of someone else."

— Judy Garland

"We do not need magic to transform our world. We carry all of the power we need inside ourselves already."

— J.K. Rowling

Understanding Affirmations

Affirmation is a term that refers to the act of affirming, agreeing to or considering something as true. In a broader psychological context, it means the regular repetition of positive statements about ourselves and the world

Affirmation has the power to reinforce our beliefs and lead to positive changes in our lives. It strengthens our faith in the truth of something and can help bring it into reality. By consciously practicing affirmation, we can even challenge and alter beliefs that were formed in our childhood.

Essentially, affirmation is the language we use to communicate with ourselves, which can be expressed through thoughts, spoken or written words. It's important to be mindful of the affirmations we use, as they shape our perception of reality. Therefore, it's crucial to cultivate a positive attitude and shift our thinking towards a more optimistic outlook on life.

The idea behind affirmations is that by repeating positive statements to ourselves, we can change our thought patterns and replace negative self-talk with positive self-talk.

Affirmations are a mental stepping outside of reality to create the future, through sentences expressed in the present.

Affirmations have a multitude of benefits

- allow you to free yourself from negative emotions;

- they enhance a sense of self-acceptance;

- help in self-development;

- in setting and achieving future goals;

- they motivate you to take action;

- change existing thought patterns.

Affirmations are a versatile tool that can be used to improve any aspect of your life. Whether you're feeling down and in need of a confidence boost, or dealing with high levels of stress or uncertainty, affirmations can be a valuable source of encouragement and positivity. However, the benefits of affirmations go beyond just helping you during difficult times. Even when you're feeling your best, affirmations can help you continue to grow and improve. For example, you can use affirmations to develop positive habits, increase your physical activity, and cultivate a greater sense of appreciation for the good things in your life. Affirmations can even help you perform better at work and increase your overall productivity. The possibilities are endless, making affirmations a powerful tool for personal growth and self-improvement.

Make your affirmations will work for You

Using affirmations on a daily basis can be an easy and effective way to incorporate positive thinking into your routine. Here are some steps you can take to make affirmations part of your daily practice.

Choose affirmations that resonate with you and align with your personal goals, values and areas you want to improve. For example, if you want to improve your self-confidence, you might choose affirmations such as "I am confident in myself and my abilities" or "I trust myself to make the right decisions."

Repeat your affirmations regularly so that they become a habit, try repeating them every day. You can say them out loud, write them down or repeat them silently in your mind. You can do this in the morning, before bed or at any other time that seems appropriate to you.

Use affirmations to reframe negative thoughts. Whenever you notice negative self-talk or limiting beliefs creeping in, try using affirmations to counter them. For example, if you think to yourself, "I'm not good enough," repeat an affirmation such as: "I am capable and worthy of success."

Incorporate affirmations into your overall self-care routine, along with other practices such as exercise, healthy eating and mindfulness. This can help you cultivate a more positive mindset and improve your overall well-being.

Easy tips and tricks for positive self -talk

Start with a clear and concise affirmation:
The first step in building a persistent positive affirmation is to craft a statement that is clear, concise, and specific. Your affirmation should be in the present tense so that your subconscious mind understands that it is a current reality rather than a future aspiration. For example, instead of saying, "I will be confident and capable," say "I am confident and capable." This way, you are telling yourself that you already possess the qualities that you desire.

Repeat your affirmation daily:
Repetition is crucial in building persistent positive affirmations. The more you repeat your affirmation, the more it becomes ingrained and reinforces the positive messages in your subconscious mind gradually reprogramming negative thinking and behavioral patterns.

Use positive language:
When creating your affirmation, it's essential to use positive language. Avoid using negative words like "don't" or "can't." Instead, focus on what you want to achieve and use positive language to reinforce it. For example, instead of saying "I don't want to be anxious," say "I am calm and relaxed." This way, you are focusing on what you want to achieve, rather than what you want to avoid.

Believe in your affirmation:
To make your affirmations more effective, it's crucial to believe in them. You must believe that your affirmation is true and achievable. If you doubt your affirmation, it won't have the desired effect.

Feel the powerful emotion of gratitude:
By feeling the powerful emotion of gratitude, you create a bridge between your intentions and the manifestation of your desires.

It's important to tap into positive emotions such as joy, contentment, happiness, and gratitude as you visualize and affirm that your desires have already become a reality. These emotions increase the effectiveness of your affirmations and align your subconscious mind with the belief that what you want is already on its way to you.

Write down your affirmation:

Writing down your affirmation can help you focus on it and remember it more easily. You can write it on a piece of paper, a sticky note, or in a journal. It's also a good idea to keep a journal to track your progress and reflect on your successes. Write down any positive changes or improvements you've noticed since you started using your affirmations.

Use affirmations for specific situations:

You can tailor your affirmations to suit specific situations. For example, if you're nervous about a presentation, your affirmation could be "I am confident and composed during my presentation." Using specific affirmations for different situations can help you feel more confident and capable in those situations.

Create a mental image of your affirmation:

Visualize yourself already achieving your goal and feel the positive emotions that come with it. See yourself as confident, capable, and successful. Try to create a vivid and detailed image of yourself embodying your affirmation.

Surround yourself with positivity:

To build persistent positive affirmations, it's important to surround yourself with positivity. You can put up inspirational posters or create a vision board with images that represent your goals and aspirations. Surrounding yourself with positivity can help you stay focused on your goals and maintain a positive mindset.

Remember, building persistent positive affirmations takes time and effort. Consistency is key, so make it a daily habit and be patient with yourself. With practice, you'll begin to see the positive impact that affirmations can have on your life.

the power of the written word

Writing affirmations is incredibly important and can be more effective than simply repeating them. When you write, you engage your senses in a different way than when you speak or read. Writing allows you to focus on specific words, process them in your mind and then put them on paper. This activity requires more attention and focus than simply repeating the words in your mind.

Writing down affirmations can help build a stronger connection between thoughts and emotions, which is key to successful affirmation practice. Engaging the senses of sight and touch through writing can help us visualize and feel what the words are expressing. This, in turn, allows us to better understand and accept these positive beliefs.

When you write affirmations, you force your mind to focus on positive thoughts for an extended period of time. This helps reinforce those positive beliefs in your psyche and solidify them in your subconscious. Therefore, writing affirmations can be a very effective practice for strengthening your positive thinking and achieving your goals.

It's wonderful that you're taking the first step towards cultivating a positive attitude and transforming your thoughts and emotions through affirmations! This shows your deep commitment to personal growth and well-being.

To help you begin this process, I've gathered together a collection of affirmations that are specifically designed to enhance different areas of your life. Choose the ones that resonate most with you and rewrite them in a way that feels authentic and empowering. Use them as a template when creating your own affirmations.

Remember that the key is repetition. Make a habit of reciting or writing them every morning upon waking up to start your day, or even before going to bed, to root them deeper within yourself and reinforce their effect. Over time, you'll begin to see changes in your thoughts, emotions and actions, and you'll begin to believe in your own power and potential.

I want to remind you that you are the mistress of your own reality, you influence it through your thoughts and feelings , which consequently create matter.You are the one who has the creative ability to shape your thoughts, feelings and experiences, and affirmations are a powerful tool to help you do that.

So take a moment to appreciate the amazing woman you are and all that you have to offer the world. Embrace the power of affirmations and know that you have a natural gift to nurture and create.

So take a deep breath, grab a pen and start your journey towards a more positive and fulfilling life. I believe in you and wish you all the best on your path.

Keep going, grow and shine!

Happiness

I AM A POWERFUL AND HAPPY WOMAN WHO ATTRACTS ABUNDANCE, LOVE, AND JOY INTO MY LIFE.

I DESERVE HAPPINESS AND JOY IN MY LIFE AND WELCOME IT WITH OPEN ARMS.

I CREATE MY OWN **HAPPINESS** THROUGH MY THOUGHTS, ACTIONS, AND ATTITUDES.

I SEE SO MANY POSITIVES IN MY LIFE.

I FIND JOY AND HAPPINESS IN EVEN THE SMALLEST
MOMENTS AND EXPERIENCES.

I AM WORTHY OF HAPPINESS AND ALL THE GOOD THINGS
LIFE HAS TO OFFER.

TODAY IS A GIFT, AND I EMBRACE IT WITH POSITIVITY.

MY HAPPINESS IS REFLECTED BACK TO ME IN
EVERYTHING I ATTRACT.

I HOLD THE KEY TO MY OWN HAPPINESS.

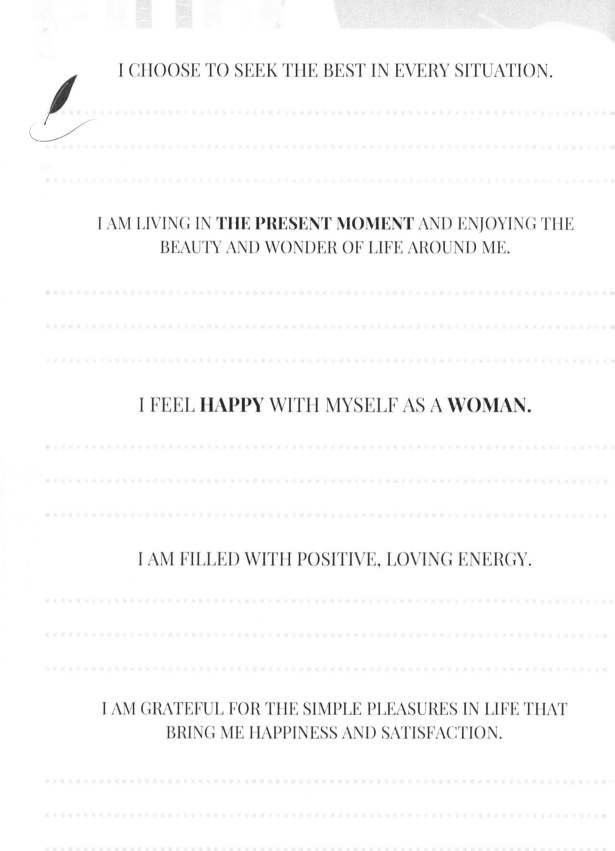

I CHOOSE TO SEEK THE BEST IN EVERY SITUATION.

I AM LIVING IN **THE PRESENT MOMENT** AND ENJOYING THE BEAUTY AND WONDER OF LIFE AROUND ME.

I FEEL **HAPPY** WITH MYSELF AS A **WOMAN.**

I AM FILLED WITH POSITIVE, LOVING ENERGY.

I AM GRATEFUL FOR THE SIMPLE PLEASURES IN LIFE THAT BRING ME HAPPINESS AND SATISFACTION.

I AM LIVING **IN BLISS.**

WHEN I EMBRACE JOY, EVERYTHING ELSE IN MY LIFE FALLS IN PLACE.

MY PRESENCE IS UPLIFTING AND JOYFUL TO OTHERS.

THE LIFE I'VE ALWAYS DREAMED OF IS CREATED BY MY CHOICE TO BE JOYFUL.

I DELIGHT IN THE SMALL WONDERS I AM BLESSED WITH.

SMILES FILL **MY HEART WITH JOY.**

I SET MY INTENTION TO ENJOY TODAY AND EVERY DAY.

WHEN I FEEL HAPPY I MANIFEST MORE REASONS TO
BE HAPPY.

THE HAPPINESS I FEEL IS FELT BY EVERYONE AROUND ME.

I FOCUS ON THE PRESENT MOMENT AND FIND JOY IN THE
LITTLE THINGS THAT **MAKE LIFE WORTH LIVING.**

HAPPINESS IS A CHOICE, AND **I CHOOSE TO BE HAPPY** EVERY DAY.

MY LIFE IS FILLED WITH JOY, LAUGHTER, AND POSITIVITY.

MY FEMININITY AND INTELLIGENCE SHINE WITH BRIGHTNESS.

I LIVE THE BEST LIFE, IN THE BEST HOME, WITH THE LOVE OF MY LIFE.

I AM TRUE TO MYSELF AND LIVE A LIFE IN ALIGNMENT WITH MY VALUES AND PASSIONS.

I FEEL GRATITUDE FOR THE WONDERFUL THINGS IN MY LIFE.

I FOCUS ON THE GOOD IN MY LIFE INSTEAD OF DWELLING ON THE NEGATIVE.

I AM WORTHY AND DESERVING OF MY BEAUTIFUL DREAMS.

I HAVE EVERYTHING I NEED.

I CREATE A BEAUTIFUL LIFE FILLED WITH LIMITLESS ABUNDANCE.

HAPPINESS DOES NOT DEPEND ON EXTERNAL CONDITIONS BUT
ON MY INNER STATE AND PERSPECTIVE.

I APPROACH EACH DAY WITH JOY AND EXCITEMENT.

I AM WILLING **TO BE HAPPY NOW**.

I HAVE THE POWER TO CREATE MY OWN HAPPINESS.

I AM AT PEACE WITH MY PAST, AND I AM IN LOVE WITH
MY PRESENT.

MY INNER JOY IS INFINITE, LIMITLESS, AND ABUNDANT.

SUCCESS IS NOT THE KEY TO MY HAPPINESS;
HAPPINESS IS THE KEY TO MY SUCCESS.

I CONCENTRATE MY THOUGHTS ON IDEAS AND BELIEFS
THAT MAKE ME FEEL GOOD.

TODAY I WILL BE **FABULOUS.**

I AM THANKFUL FOR WHAT I HAVE, EVEN IF IT IS
NOT PERFECT.

I DESERVE EVERYTHING I WANT IN LIFE.

WHEN I FOCUS ON GRATITUDE, HAPPINESS FLOWS
TO ME EASILY.

HAPPINESS IS MY NATURAL STATE OF BEING, AND I
ALLOW IT TO FLOW FREELY WITHIN ME.

I FIND PLEASURE IN THE LITTLE MOMENTS.

I AM GRATEFUL FOR THE MAGIC AND MIRACLES THAT
LIFE BRINGS ME.

I TRUST THE UNIVERSE WILL HELP ME LIVE MY BEST LIFE.

GRATITUDE IS THE BRIDGE TO A LIFE OF JOY, PEACE, AND ABUNDANCE.

MY LIFE IS WONDERFUL AND EVERYTHING IS WORKING OUT IN A PERFECT WAY FOR ME.

JOY IS THE ESSENCE OF MY BEING.

I AM APPRECIATING EVERY BLESSING, NO MATTER HOW SMALL.

WONDERFUL THINGS ARE GOING TO HAPPEN TO ME.

I AM NOT MY PAST AND I'M CAPABLE OF CREATING A
BETTER FUTURE.

I HAVE EVERYTHING I NEED TO WORK TOWARDS
BECOMING HAPPIER.

I REFUSE TO LET OTHER PEOPLE'S OPINIONS
AFFECT MY HAPPINESS.

THE UNIVERSE HAS MY BEST INTEREST AT HEART, AND
EVERYTHING HAPPENS FOR MY HIGHEST GOOD.

"the most important thing is to enjoy your life - to be happy - it's all that matters." - Audrey Hepburn

"The happiness of your life depends upon the quality of your thoughts." - Aristotle

"Optimism is a happiness magnet. If you stay positive, good things and good people will be drawn to you" - Mary Lou Retton

"the purpose of our lifes is to be happy" -Dalai Lama

"The art of being happy lies in the power of extracting happiness from common things"-Henry Ward Beecher

"Happiness is not a state to arrive at, but a manner of traveling." - Margaret Lee Runbeck

"If you want to be happy, be"- Leo Tolstoy

Every day is a new day" -Carrie Underwood

Start each day with a grateful heart.

"Count your age by friends, not years. Count your life by smiles, not tears." -John Lenon

"Being happy never goes out of style" -Lilly Pulitzer

"Thousands of candles can be lighted from a single candle, and the life of the candle will not be shortened. Happiness never decreases by being shared."-Buddha

Close your eyes, take a deep breath, and focus on the things that bring you joy and contentment. Visualize a life filled with happiness and positivity, take your time to reflect on your blessings and write affirmations from your heart. Remember that true happiness is within your reach, and you have the power to create it in your life.

Self-Esteem

I AM WORTHY OF LOVE AND RESPECT **JUST AS I AM.**

I BELIEVE IN MY ABILITIES AND STRENGTHS.

I TRUST AND VALUE MYSELF.

I AM UNIQUE AND VALUABLE.

I AM PROUD OF MY ACCOMPLISHMENTS AND
ACHIEVEMENTS.

I AM CONFIDENT IN MY OWN SKIN AND **EMBRACE MY
IMPERFECTIONS.**

I AM GRATEFUL FOR ALL THAT I HAVE AND ALL
THAT I AM.

I AM PROUD OF THE WOMAN I AM BECOMING.

I HAVE FAITH IN MYSELF AND MAKE CHOICES THAT ARE IN
LINE WITH MY VALUES AND BELIEFS.

I LET GO OF NEGATIVE SELF-TALK AND REPLACE IT WITH **POSITIVE AFFIRMATIONS.**

I AM LEARNING AND GROWING EVERY DAY.

I AM KIND AND COMPASSIONATE TOWARDS MYSELF AND OTHERS.

I AM PROUD OF WHO I AM AND WHAT I HAVE ACCOMPLISHED.

I TRUST MYSELF TO MAKE DECISIONS THAT ALIGN WITH MY BEST INTERESTS.

I AM SPECIAL AND UNIQUE. THERE'S NO ONE ELSE LIKE ME.

I SAY GOODBYE TO SELF-CRITICISM AND ALL FEARS.

I LOVE MYSELF MORE AND MORE EACH DAY.

I HAVE THE POWER TO **CREATE THE LIFE I WANT.**

I AM BEAUTIFUL, INTELLIGENT, FUN, AND FULL OF LIFE.

I AM ENOUGH JUST AS I AM.

I AM DESERVING OF HAPPINESS AND FULFILLMENT IN ALL
AREAS OF MY LIFE.

I CHOOSE TO LET GO OF SELF-DOUBT AND EMBRACE SELF-
CONFIDENCE.

I AM WORTHY OF RESPECT AND BOUNDARIES IN ALL OF MY
RELATIONSHIPS.

I CELEBRATE MY STRENGTHS AND RECOGNIZE MY AREAS
OF GROWTH.

I AM RESILIENT AND CAPABLE OF OVERCOMING ANY
CHALLENGE.

I AM DESERVING OF LOVE AND POSITIVE EXPERIENCES.

PEOPLE VALUE MY WORK, MY TIME, AND MY LOVE.

I CHOOSE TO **FOCUS ON MY OWN JOURNEY** AND NOT
COMPARE MYSELF TO OTHERS.

I AM WORTHY OF TAKING UP SPACE AND BEING SEEN AND
HEARD.

NOTHING CAN STOP ME FROM ACHIEVING MY DREAMS.

MY VOICE IS IMPORTANT.

I AM CONFIDENT IN MY OWN OPINIONS AND DECISIONS, AND I TRUST IN MY INTUITION.

THERE'S NOTHING I NEED TO DO OR BE TO EARN LOVE OR RESPECT.

I AM CAPABLE OF OVERCOMING CHALLENGES AND SETBACKS WITH RESILIENCE AND DETERMINATION.

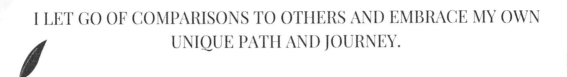

I LET GO OF COMPARISONS TO OTHERS AND EMBRACE MY OWN
UNIQUE PATH AND JOURNEY.

I LEARN AND GROW FROM MY MISTAKES, WHICH BUILDS
MY CONFIDENCE.

EVERYTHING IS POSSIBLE FOR ME.

I AM ABLE TO EXPRESS MYSELF AUTHENTICALLY AND
CREATIVELY.

MY BRAVERY SHINES IN EVERY ACT AND EVERY DECISION.

I GAIN MORE EXPERIENCE AND MORE WISDOM AS I AGE.

I HAVE EVERYTHING I NEED TO SUCCEED.

I STAND PROUDLY **IN MY TRUTH**.

I CELEBRATE MY ACHIEVEMENTS AND ACCOMPLISHMENTS, NO
MATTER HOW SMALL THEY ARE.

I CAN'T CHANGE WHAT OTHERS THINK OF ME, BUT I
CAN CHOOSE HOW I RESPOND.

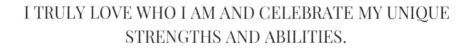

I TRULY LOVE WHO I AM AND CELEBRATE MY UNIQUE
STRENGTHS AND ABILITIES.

I AM CAPABLE OF ACHIEVING MY GOALS AND DREAMS, AND I
TRUST IN **MY OWN ABILITIES AND POTENTIAL.**

I AM WORTHY OF SUCCESS AND HAPPINESS, AND **I TAKE
ACTION** TOWARDS THESE GOALS EVERY DAY.

NOTHING IS MORE POWERFUL THAN MY BELIEF IN ME.

EACH DAY I AM MORE & MORE AWARE OF MY INNATE BEAUTY,
CREATIVITY & ABUNDANCE.

I BELIEVE IN MY ABILITY TO EXPRESS MY TRUE SELF
WITH EASE.

I AM SHAPING THE LIFE THAT'S WAITING FOR ME.

THERE'S **NOTHING** I NEED **TO CHANGE** ABOUT MYSELF TO BE
ACCEPTED AND LOVED.

I CAN ASSERT MYSELF AND **STAND UP** FOR MYSELF
AND OTHERS.

I LOVE WHO I AM AND WHO I AM BECOMING.

I TRUST IN MY OWN ABILITIES AND STRENGTHS, AND I USE THEM TO MAKE A POSITIVE DIFFERENCE IN THE WORLD.

I RELEASE THE NEED FOR EXTERNAL VALIDATION AND EMBRACE MY OWN SENSE OF WORTH AND ESTEEM.

I ACKNOWLEDGE MY OWN SELF-WORTH – MY CONFIDENCE IS RISING.

I AM WORTHY OF RESPECT AND DIGNITY, AND I CHOOSE TO TREAT MYSELF WITH RESPECT AND DIGNITY.

I AM READY TO TAKE MY **LIFE IN MY HANDS.**

"Remember always that you not only have the right to be an individual, you have an obligation to be one." - Eleanor Roosevelt

Never forget your worth.

"Wanting to be someone else is a waste of the person you are."
Marilyn Monroe

"DON'T BACK DOWN JUST TO KEEP THE PEACE. STANDING UP FOR YOUR BELIEFS BUILDS SELF-CONFIDENCE AND SELF-ESTEEM."
~ OPRAH WINFREY

"the greatest thing in the world is to know how to belong to oneself."
Michel de Montaigne

"Love yourself first and everything else falls into line. You really have to love yourself to get anything done in this world." -- Lucille Ball

"Believe in your infinite potential. Your only limitations are those you set upon yourself."
- Roy T. Bennett

"Act as if what you do makes a difference. It does." – William James

"REMEMBER, YOU HAVE BEEN CRITICIZING YOURSELF FOR YEARS, AND IT HASN'T WORKED. TRY APPROVING OF YOURSELF AND SEE WHAT HAPPENS."
– LOUISE L. HAY

"You're always with yourself, so you might as well enjoy the company.
- Diane Von Furstenberg

Start by acknowledging your strengths and accomplishments. Take a deep breath and visualize a version of yourself that is confident and self-assured. Write down affirmations that reflect your worth and value. Remember that you are worthy of love, respect, and success, and that your unique qualities make you a valuable contribution to the world.

Self-Image & Body

I AM BEAUTIFUL, INSIDE AND OUT.

I CHOOSE TO SEE MYSELF THROUGH A LENS OF
POSITIVITY AND SELF-LOVE.

I AM PROUD OF MY PHYSICAL FEATURES AND
APPRECIATE THEM FOR WHAT THEY ARE.

I RELEASE THE NEED TO COMPARE MYSELF TO OTHERS
AND EMBRACE MY UNIQUE BEAUTY.

I LOVE AND ACCEPT MY BODY AS IT IS, RIGHT NOW.

MY WORTH IS NOT DETERMINED BY HOW I LOOK.

MY BODY IS WORTHY OF LOVE AND RESPECT,
REGARDLESS OF ITS SIZE OR SHAPE.

I AM **MORE** THAN JUST MY PHYSICAL APPEARANCE.

MY BODY IS A BEAUTIFUL AND UNIQUE
EXPRESSION OF WHO I AM.

I AM FEELING GOOD ABOUT MYSELF.

I DESERVE TO FEEL CONFIDENT AND BEAUTIFUL
IN MY OWN SKIN.

I AM WORTHY OF LOVE AND ACCEPTANCE, REGARDLESS
OF MY APPEARANCE.

I AM GRATEFUL FOR MY BODY AND ALL THAT IT
ALLOWS ME TO DO.

I CELEBRATE MY NATURAL BEAUTY AND EMBRACE
MY IMPERFECTIONS.

I CHOOSE TO FOCUS ON WHAT **MY BODY CAN DO**,
RATHER THAN HOW IT LOOKS.

I AM DESERVING OF LOVE AND HAPPINESS,
REGARDLESS OF **MY BODY TYPE.**

I TRUST MY BODY'S NATURAL INSTINCTS AND NEEDS.

MY BODY DESERVES TO BE NOURISHED WITH **HEALTHY**
FOODS AND EXERCISE.

I GIVE MYSELF PERMISSION TO WEAR WHAT I WANT,
REGARDLESS OF SOCIETAL STANDARDS.

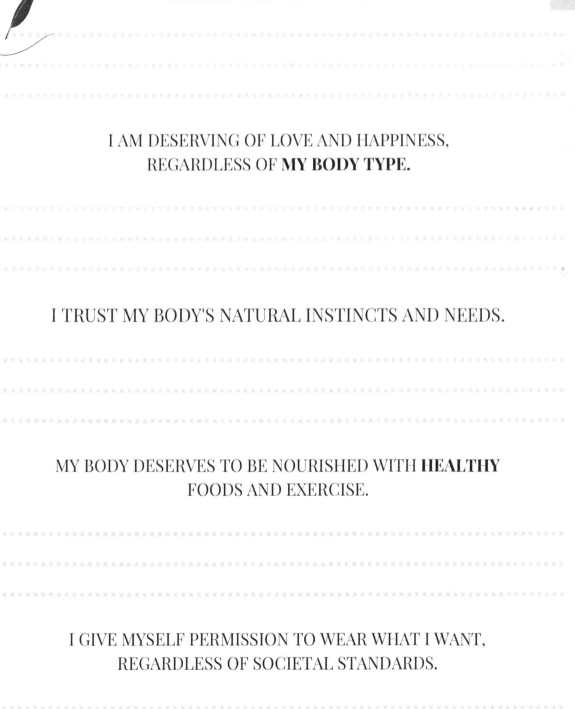

I RELEASE THE NEED TO CONFORM TO SOCIETAL BEAUTY STANDARDS AND **EMBRACE MY INDIVIDUALITY.**

I CHOOSE TO NOURISH MY BODY WITH HEALTHY FOODS AND EXERCISE, RATHER THAN OBSESS OVER MY APPEARANCE.

I AM COMFORTABLE EXPRESSING MYSELF THROUGH MY PERSONAL STYLE.

I TRUST MY OWN INTUITION WHEN IT COMES TO TAKING CARE OF MY APPEARANCE.

I AM ALLOWED TO EXPERIMENT WITH DIFFERENT HAIRSTYLES, MAKEUP, AND FASHION CHOICES.

I AM ALLOWED TO TAKE UP SPACE AND **EXIST IN THIS WORLD,**
JUST **AS I AM.**

I EMBRACE MY CURVES AND **LOVE EVERY INCH** OF MY BODY.

I AM BEAUTIFUL, JUST AS I AM.

I RELEASE NEGATIVE SELF-TALK ABOUT MY BODY AND REPLACE IT WITH POSITIVE AFFIRMATIONS.

I APPRECIATE MY BODY FOR ALL THAT IT DOES FOR ME.

I TRUST THAT **MY** UNIQUE **BEAUTY SHINES** FROM WITHIN,
REGARDLESS OF MY OUTWARD APPEARANCE.

I AM BEAUTIFUL, REGARDLESS OF WHAT OTHERS MAY
SAY OR THINK.

I EMBRACE MY OWN JOURNEY OF SELF-
DISCOVERY AND SELF-LOVE.

I AM ACCEPTING MYSELF AS I AM RIGHT NOW.

I AM ALLOWED TO AGE GRACEFULLY AND APPRECIATE THE
CHANGES THAT COME WITH TIME.

I AM FEELING **FABULOUS** AND **CONFIDENT** IN MY BODY.

I REJECT THE IDEA THAT MY BODY NEEDS TO BE CHANGED
TO FIT INTO SOCIETAL STANDARDS OF BEAUTY.

MY BODY DESERVES TO BE TREATED WITH **KINDNESS AND CARE**.

I AM GRATEFUL FOR THE UNIQUE QUALITIES AND
FEATURES THAT MAKE ME WHO I AM.

I AM PROUD OF **MY BODY** AND ALL THAT IT **HAS OVERCOME**.

I AM ALLOWED TO INDULGE IN THE FOODS THAT BRING
ME JOY AND PLEASURE.

I PROMISE TO **LOVE AND CHERISH** MY BODY.

I CELEBRATE MY BODY'S VICTORIES, NO
MATTER HOW SMALL.

I ENJOY WORKING OUT TO KEEP MY BODY FIT.

I TRUST MY BODY'S INNATE **ABILITY TO HEAL** AND THRIVE.

I APPRECIATE MY BODY FOR ALL THAT IT DOES FOR
ME, BOTH PHYSICALLY AND AESTHETICALLY.

MY BODY IS MY GREATEST **GIFT,** AND I TREAT IT WELL.

I CHOOSE TO APPRECIATE MY BODY FOR ALL THAT IT DOES FOR
ME, RATHER THAN CRITICIZE IT FOR WHAT IT DOESN'T.

I AM PERFECT, WHOLE, AND **COMPLETE** JUST THE WAY I AM.

THERE IS MORE TO LIFE THAT WORRYING ABOUT MY
WEIGHT. I'M READY TO EXPERIENCE IT.

I AM DESERVING OF COMPLIMENTS AND ADMIRATION FOR MY BEAUTY AND INNER QUALITIES.

A GOAL WEIGHT IS AN ARBITRARY NUMBER; **HOW I FEEL IS** WHAT'S **IMPORTANT**.

I AM BEAUTIFUL, NO MATTER WHAT STAGE OF LIFE I AM IN.

I AM PROUD OF THE WAY I PRESENT MYSELF TO THE WORLD.

I AM ALLOWED TO **PRIORITIZE MY OWN SELF-CARE** AND BEAUTY ROUTINES.

I AM ALLOWED TO INDULGE IN SELF-CARE PRACTICES THAT
MAKE ME FEEL BEAUTIFUL AND CONFIDENT.

NO ONE HAS THE POWER TO MAKE ME FEEL BAD ABOUT
MYSELF **WITHOUT MY PERMISSION**.

MY BODY IS PERFECT FOR ME.

I TRUST THAT MY OWN SENSE OF BEAUTY **IS
VALID** AND WORTHY.

I AM WORTHY OF BEING SEEN AND APPRECIATED
FOR MY UNIQUE BEAUTY.

"I am beginning to measure myself in strength, not pounds. Sometimes in smiles."
— Laurie Halse Anderson

You are Beautiful

"BEAUTY BEGINS THE MOMENT YOU DECIDE TO BE YOURSELF."
- COCO CHANEL

"A strong, positive self-image is the best possible preparation for success." Joyce Brothers

"It's not what you say out of your mouth that determines your life, it's what you whisper to yourself that has the most power!
— Robert T. Kiyosaki

YOU ARE AMAZING

"Mirrors are perpetually deceitful. They lie and steal your true self. They reveal only what your mind believes it sees"
— Dee Remy

"Love yourself. It is important to stay positive because beauty comes from the inside out."
-Jenn Proske

IN CASE YOU FORGOT TO REMIND YOURSELF THIS MORNING... YOUR BUTT IS PERFECT. YOUR SMILE LIGHTS UP THE ROOM. YOUR MIND IS INSANELY COOL. YOU ARE MORE THAN ENOUGH. AND YOU ARE DOING AN AMAZING JOB AT LIFE."
-L.K. ELLIOTT

"Beauty is when you can appreciate yourself. When you love yourself, that's when you're most **beautiful.**" Zoe Kravitz

Your journey is unique and valuable. Close your eyes and visualize a version of yourself that is confident and comfortable in your own skin. Write your affirmations with authenticity and vulnerability recognizing the unique qualities and beauty that you possess.

Self-Worth & Dignity

I HAVE THE RIGHT TO **REFUSE** ANY REQUEST THAT DOES NOT
ALIGN WITH MY VALUES OR PRIORITIES.

I HAVE THE COURAGE AND **POWER TO SAY "NO."**

I TRUST MYSELF TO MAKE DECISIONS THAT HONOR MY NEEDS
AND RESPECT MY BOUNDARIES, EVEN IF IT MEANS REFUSING
OTHERS.

I HAVE THE RIGHT TO BE TREATED **WITH
RESPECT AND DIGNITY.**

I BELIEVE IN THE **INHERENT WORTH AND VALUE OF ALL WOMEN,** REGARDLESS OF THEIR BACKGROUND OR CIRCUMSTANCES.

I ACKNOWLEDGE MY STRENGTHS AND ABILITIES AND WILL **NOT ALLOW** ANYONE **TO DIMINISH THEM.**

I SUPPORT AND **STAND WITH WOMEN** WHO ARE FIGHTING FOR THEIR RIGHTS AND DIGNITY AROUND THE WORLD.

I BELIEVE IN MY OWN WORTH AND WILL NOT LET ANYONE ELSE DEFINE IT FOR ME.

I AM CAPABLE OF SETTING BOUNDARIES AND COMMUNICATING MY NEEDS IN A CLEAR AND RESPECTFUL WAY.

I KNOW MY OWN WORTH AND WILL NOT LET ANYONE
ELSE DIMINISH IT.

I TRUST MY OWN JUDGMENT AND INTUITION AND WILL MAKE
DECISIONS THAT **HONOR MY SELF-WORTH.**

I AM VALUABLE AND WORTHY SIMPLY BECAUSE I EXIST.

I DESERVE TO BE TREATED WITH **RESPECT**, KINDNESS,
AND CONSIDERATION.

I WILL NOT ALLOW ANYONE TO MAKE ME FEEL
INFERIOR OR UNWORTHY.

I WILL NOT ALLOW ANYONE TO TREAT ME IN A WAY THAT
UNDERMINES MY DIGNITY OR SELF-WORTH.

I CHOOSE TO PRESERVE **MY DIGNITY BEFORE** OTHERS.

MY VOICE AND OPINIONS ARE VALUABLE AND SHOULD BE
HEARD AND RESPECTED.

I REJECT ALL FORMS OF VIOLENCE, DISCRIMINATION, AND
OPPRESSION AGAINST WOMEN.

I RECOGNIZE THAT **MY WORTH AS A WOMAN** IS NOT BASED ON
EXTERNAL FACTORS SUCH AS APPEARANCE OR ACHIEVEMENTS.

I AM CAPABLE OF MAKING CHOICES THAT ALIGN WITH **MY VALUES AND BELIEFS.**

I WILL NOT JUDGE OR SHAME MYSELF FOR PAST CHOICES, BUT INSTEAD LEARN FROM THEM.

I WILL NOT ALLOW OTHERS TO SHAME OR CRITICIZE ME FOR **MY CHOICES.**

I WILL NOT FEEL GUILTY FOR PRIORITIZING MY OWN NEEDS AND DESIRES WHEN MAKING CHOICES.

I REFUSE TO LET OTHERS PRESSURE OR COERCE ME INTO CHOICES THAT DO NOT ALIGN WITH MY VALUES AND DESIRES.

I HAVE THE **RIGHT TO SPEAK UP AND ADVOCATE** FOR
MYSELF AND OTHERS.

MY **IDENTITY** AND **DIVERSITY** ARE SOURCES OF
STRENGTH AND SHOULD BE CELEBRATED.

MY VOICE MATTERS, AND I HAVE THE RIGHT TO BE HEARD.

I HAVE THE RIGHT TO SPEAK UP FOR MYSELF
AND ASSERT MY NEEDS AND WANTS.

I ACKNOWLEDGE AND **RESPECT MY OWN BOUNDARIES** AND LIMITS.

I AM DESERVING OF EQUAL TREATMENT AND OPPORTUNITIES,
REGARDLESS OF MY GENDER.

I BELIEVE THAT WOMEN'S RIGHTS ARE **HUMAN RIGHTS**
AND SHOULD BE UNIVERSALLY **PROTECTED.**

I AM CAPABLE OF STANDING UP FOR MYSELF IN THE FACE OF
DISCRIMINATION OR INJUSTICE.

I HAVE **STRONG FAITH** IN MYSELF.

I WILL NOT LET ANYONE DISMISS OR BELITTLE MY
EXPERIENCES OR **EMOTIONS.**

I AM CAPABLE OF TAKING CARE OF MYSELF AND MAKING
MY **OWN DECISIONS.**

I WILL NOT ALLOW ANYONE TO MAKE ME FEEL
INFERIOR OR LESS THAN.

I RECOGNIZE AND APPRECIATE THE **VALUE THAT I BRING TO
THE WORLD** AND TO THOSE AROUND ME.

I AM DESERVING OF RESPECT AND DIGNITY IN ALL OF
MY RELATIONSHIPS.

I WILL NOT LET ANYONE ELSE DEFINE MY WORTH
OR DETERMINE MY PATH IN LIFE.

I WILL NOT ALLOW ANYONE TO MAKE ME FEEL ASHAMED
OF MY BODY OR APPEARANCE.

I DESERVE TO BE TREATED WITH **KINDNESS AND
EMPATHY**, EVEN WHEN I MAKE MISTAKES.

I WILL NOT LET ANYONE UNDERMINE MY CONFIDENCE
OR SELF-ESTEEM.

I RECOGNIZE AND RESPECT THE DIGNITY AND WORTH OF
OTHERS, REGARDLESS OF **THEIR DIFFERENCES.**

I AM DESERVING OF COMPASSION AND UNDERSTANDING
FROM MYSELF AND OTHERS.

I HAVE THE RIGHT TO **EXPRESS** MY THOUGHTS, FEELINGS, AND OPINIONS **WITHOUT FEAR** OF JUDGMENT OR CRITICISM.

I AM CAPABLE OF CREATING HEALTHY AND SUPPORTIVE RELATIONSHIPS IN MY LIFE.

MY WORTH AS A PERSON IS NOT BASED ON WHAT I DO OR HOW MUCH I HAVE.

I DESERVE LOVE, CARE AND COMPASSION FROM MYSELF, MY FRIENDS AND FAMILY.

I AM PROUD OF WHAT AND WHERE I AM TODAY.

I RECOGNIZE AND APPRECIATE **THE UNIQUE QUALITIES**
THAT MAKE ME WHO I AM.

I WILL NOT ALLOW ANYONE TO MAKE ME FEEL LIKE I
AM NOT GOOD ENOUGH.

I DESERVE TO BE TREATED WITH KINDNESS, EMPATHY,
AND UNDERSTANDING.

I WILL NOT COMPARE MYSELF TO OTHERS OR BASE MY WORTH ON
EXTERNAL FACTORS SUCH AS APPEARANCE OR STATUS.

I AM GRATEFUL FOR THE FREEDOM TO MAKE CHOICES AND
CREATE MY OWN PATH IN LIFE.

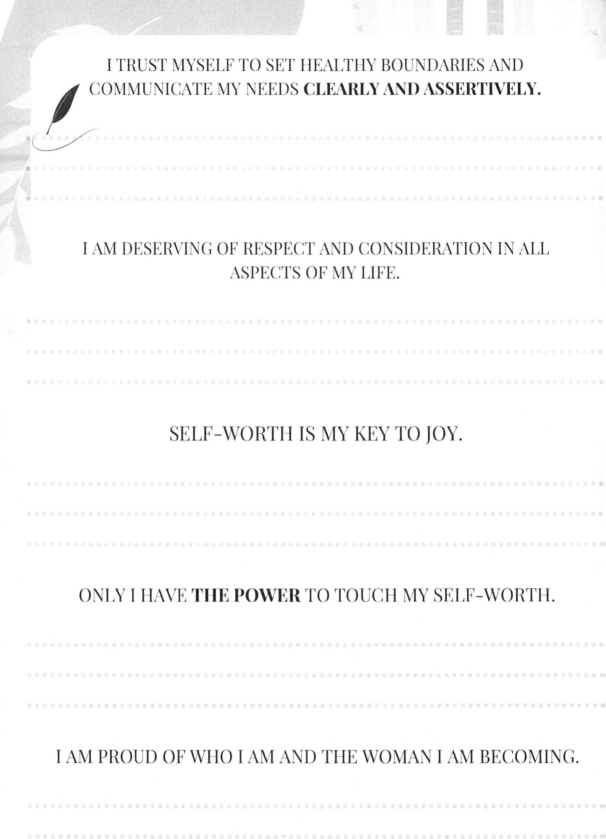

I TRUST MYSELF TO SET HEALTHY BOUNDARIES AND COMMUNICATE MY NEEDS **CLEARLY AND ASSERTIVELY.**

I AM DESERVING OF RESPECT AND CONSIDERATION IN ALL ASPECTS OF MY LIFE.

SELF-WORTH IS MY KEY TO JOY.

ONLY I HAVE **THE POWER** TO TOUCH MY SELF-WORTH.

I AM PROUD OF WHO I AM AND THE WOMAN I AM BECOMING.

YOUR WORTH IS NOT MEASURED BY THE OPINIONS OF OTHERS, BUT BY THE VALUE YOU PLACE ON YOURSELF." - UNKNOWN

"The most powerful relationship you will ever have is the relationship with yourself." - Steve Maraboli

"I don't care what you think of me. I don't think of you at all." Coco Chanel

"You yourself, as much as anybody in the entire universe, deserve your love and affection."- Buddha

"Self-respect, self-worth, and self-love, all start with self. Stop looking outside of yourself for your value." - Rob Liano

"Self-worth comes from one thing - thinking that you are worthy." - Wayne Dyer

"Your value doesn't decrease based on someone's inability to see your worth." - Unknown

"You are not a drop in the ocean. You are the entire ocean in a drop." - Rumi

"NO ONE CAN DIMINISH OUR VALUE UNLESS WE LET THEM." —ROSALIND SEDACCA

"No one can make you feel inferior without your consent." - Eleanor Roosevelt

"Respect yourself above all." —Pythagoras

"You are valuable because you exist. Not because of what you do or what you have done, but simply because you are." - Max Lucado

"Don't let the world tell you that you are not enough. You are enough, just as you are." - Unknown

71

Your thoughts and words have immense power.
Start by recognizing your inherent worth as a human being,
regardless of external circumstances or the opinions of others. Write
your affirmations, knowing that you have the right to be treated with
respect and dignity, both by yourself and by others.

Confidence

I AM CONFIDENT IN MY ABILITIES AND TRUST IN MY OWN JUDGMENT.

I AM CAPABLE OF HANDLING ANY CHALLENGES THAT COME MY WAY **WITH RESILIENCE AND DETERMINATION.**

I AM CONFIDENT IN MY OWN UNIQUE QUALITIES AND **EMBRACE MY INDIVIDUALITY.**

REGARDLESS OF THE SITUATION, I FEEL IMMENSE SELF-CONFIDENCE.

I CHOOSE TO FOCUS ON **THE PRESENT MOMENT** AND BELIEVE
IN MY ABILITY TO CREATE A **POSITIVE FUTURE.**

I AM WORTHY OF LOVE AND ACCEPTANCE, AND I TREAT MYSELF
WITH THE SAME KINDNESS I WOULD OFFER TO A LOVED ONE.

I CAN LET GO OF MY INSECURITIES.

I AM CONFIDENT IN MY ABILITY TO HANDLE UNCERTAINTY
AND CHANGE WITH GRACE AND EASE.

I AM CAPABLE OF FACING ANY CHALLENGE WITH COURAGE
AND DETERMINATION.

I RELEASE SELF-DOUBT AND EMBRACE **UNSHAKEABLE CONFIDENCE AND SELF-BELIEF.**

I DESERVE THE BEST THINGS THAT THIS WORLD HAS TO OFFER.

I TRUST IN MY OWN INSTINCTS AND ABILITY TO MAKE **WISE DECISIONS.**

I AM CONFIDENT IN MY ABILITY TO COMMUNICATE EFFECTIVELY AND ASSERTIVELY.

I **FEEL EXTREME CONFIDENCE** IN EVERY AREA OF MY LIFE.

I CHOOSE TO FOCUS ON MY STRENGTHS AND USE THEM
TO ACHIEVE MY GOALS.

I AM COMFORTABLE WITH WHO I AM AND I DON'T NEED
VALIDATION FROM OTHERS.

I AM **THE MOST AMAZING WOMAN**, AND I
BELIEVE IT WITH ALL MY BEING.

I AM CREATED TO BE OUTSTANDING.

WHEN I LOOK IN THE MIRROR, **I LOVE** THE WONDERFUL
AND POWERFUL **WOMAN STARING BACK AT ME.**

I TRUST MYSELF COMPLETELY. THE STRENGTH I NEED
IS WITHIN ME.

I AM WORTHY OF BEING CONFIDENT IN ALL AREAS OF MY LIFE.

I AM A PRODUCT OF MY THOUGHTS, I BECOME
WHAT I THINK.

I AM WORTHY OF PURSUING MY PASSIONS AND
LIVING **A FULFILLING LIFE.**

I AM CONSTANTLY FINDING WAYS TO CHALLENGE
AND PUSH MYSELF TO NEW HEIGHTS.

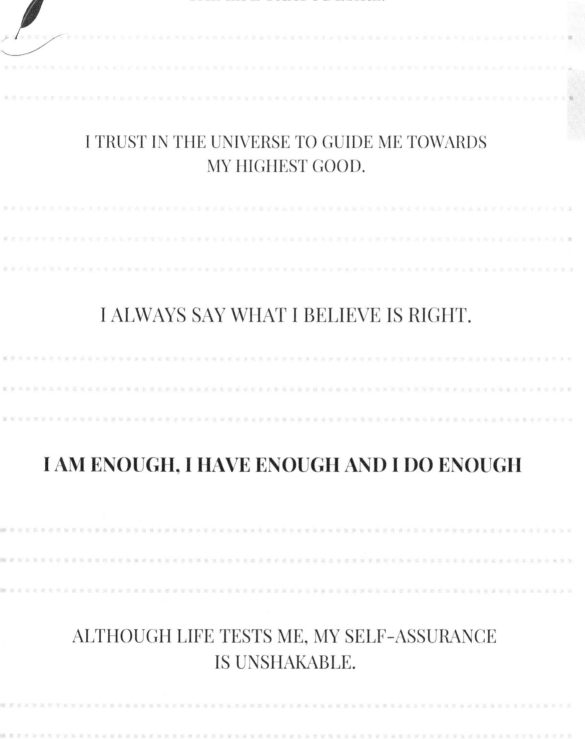

I AM CONFIDENT IN MY ABILITY TO CREATE
THE LIFE THAT I DESIRE.

I TRUST IN THE UNIVERSE TO GUIDE ME TOWARDS
MY HIGHEST GOOD.

I ALWAYS SAY WHAT I BELIEVE IS RIGHT.

I AM ENOUGH, I HAVE ENOUGH AND I DO ENOUGH

ALTHOUGH LIFE TESTS ME, MY SELF–ASSURANCE
IS UNSHAKABLE.

I AM CONFIDENT IN MY ABILITIES AND TALENTS.

I AM ONLY COMPARING MYSELF TO MY
YESTERDAY'S VERSION.

I BECOME THE MOST CONFIDENT VERSION OF MYSELF.

I AM PROUD OF HOW FAR I HAVE COME.

I HAVE ALWAYS BEEN AND WILL ALWAYS **BE GREAT,** I
FEEL IT WITH EVERY CELL OF MY BODY.

I AM **STRONGER THAN I THINK**.

IF SOMETHING DOES NOT SUIT ME, I SPEAK ABOUT IT. **I NEVER ACCEPT TACIT CONSENT.**

I KNOW I DON'T HAVE TO BE PERFECT.

I RADIATE CONFIDENCE AND ATTRACT SUCCESS IN EVERY ASPECT OF MY LIFE.

I TRUST IN MY OWN **JOURNEY** AND BELIEVE IN THE PATH I AM ON.

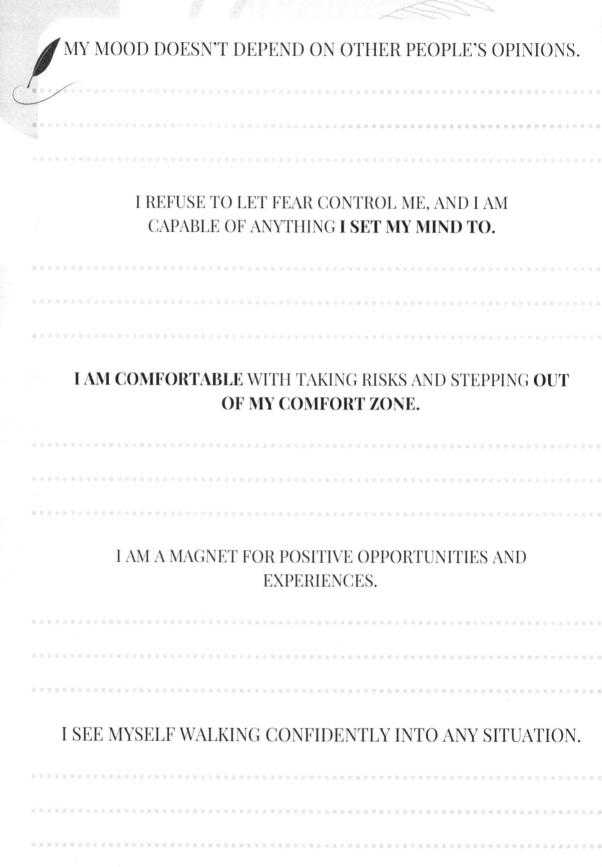

MY MOOD DOESN'T DEPEND ON OTHER PEOPLE'S OPINIONS.

I REFUSE TO LET FEAR CONTROL ME, AND I AM
CAPABLE OF ANYTHING **I SET MY MIND TO.**

I AM COMFORTABLE WITH TAKING RISKS AND STEPPING **OUT
OF MY COMFORT ZONE.**

I AM A MAGNET FOR POSITIVE OPPORTUNITIES AND
EXPERIENCES.

I SEE MYSELF WALKING CONFIDENTLY INTO ANY SITUATION.

82

I AM CONFIDENT IN MY ABILITY TO LEARN NEW THINGS AND
ADAPT TO ANY SITUATION.

I AM CAPABLE OF STANDING UP FOR MYSELF AND MY BELIEFS
WITH COURAGE AND CONVICTION.

I CHOOSE TO **FOCUS ON MY PROGRESS** RATHER THAN MY
PERCEIVED LIMITATIONS OR SETBACKS.

I AM WORTHY OF SUCCESS AND HAPPINESS, AND I BELIEVE IN MY
ABILITY TO ACHIEVE THEM.

I TRUST IN MY OWN JOURNEY AND BELIEVE IN THE INFINITE
POSSIBILITIES THAT EXIST FOR MY FUTURE.

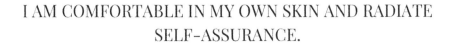

I AM COMFORTABLE IN MY OWN SKIN AND RADIATE SELF–ASSURANCE.

I AM CONSTANTLY FINDING WAYS TO BUILD MY CONFIDENCE AND SELF–ESTEEM.

MY POWER IS UNLIMITED.

I AM OPEN TO RECEIVING AND GIVING **CONSTRUCTIVE FEEDBACK.**

I AM READY TO TURN THE PAGE AND **CREATE** THE **FUTURE OF MY DREAMS.**

I DON'T HAVE TO STAY AROUND PEOPLE THAT DON'T
MAKE ME HAPPY.

I AM COMFORTABLE ACKNOWLEDGING MY **STRENGTHS AND
WEAKNESSES.**

I AM A CONFIDENT AND CHARISMATIC LEADER.

I CAN **EXPRESS** MY **EMOTIONS**.

I AM CONFIDENT IN MY ABILITY TO CREATE POSITIVE
CHANGE IN MY LIFE AND THE WORLD AROUND ME.

"Confidence comes not from always being right, but from not fearing to be wrong." - Peter T. McIntyre

"If you hear a voice within you say 'you cannot paint,' then by all means paint, and that voice will be silenced." - Vincent Van Gogh

"Trust yourself--you know more than you think you do." - Benjamin Spock

"Confidence is the sexiest thing a woman can have. It's much sexier than any body part."
- Aimee Mullins

"One important key to success is self-confidence. An important key to self-confidence is preparation."
- Arthur Ashe

"Confidence is not 'they will like me'. Confidence is 'I'll be fine if they don't'."
- Christina Grimmie

'THE MOST BEAUTIFUL THING YOU CAN WEAR IS CONFIDENCE."
- BLAKE LIVELY

"With confidence, you have won before you have started."
- Marcus Garvey

"the moment you doubt whether you can fly, you cease forever to be able to do it."
- J.M. Barrie, Peter Pan

"BELIEVE IN YOURSELF AND ALL THAT YOU ARE. KNOW THAT THERE IS SOMETHING INSIDE YOU THAT IS GREATER THAN ANY OBSTACLE."
- CHRISTIAN D. LARSON

"Man often becomes what he believes himself to be. If I keep on saying to myself that I cannot do a certain thing, it is possible that I may end by really becoming incapable of doing it. On the contrary, if I have the belief that I can do it, I shall surely acquire the capacity to do it even if I may not have it at the beginning."
- Mahatama Gandhi

Take a moment to reflect on your unique strengths, talents and abilities. Let them guide you as you write your affirmations. Remember that confidence is a mindset that can be developed and strengthened, and that you have the power to cultivate it through your thoughts, actions, and experiences.

Abundance

I AM WORTHY OF **ABUNDANCE AND PROSPERITY**, AND I KNOW THAT IT **IS WITHIN MY REACH.**

I TRUST IN THE UNIVERSE TO PROVIDE ME WITH ALL THAT I NEED TO LIVE A FULFILLING AND ABUNDANT LIFE.

I AM CONFIDENT IN MY ABILITY TO CREATE WEALTH AND **ABUNDANCE IN ALL AREAS OF MY LIFE.**

I AM CAPABLE OF MANIFESTING MY DESIRES THROUGH VISUALIZATION AND POSITIVE AFFIRMATIONS.

I RELEASE LIMITING BELIEFS ABOUT MONEY AND
EMBRACE A **MINDSET OF ABUNDANCE.**

I AM ABUNDANT IN ALL AREAS OF MY LIFE, INCLUDING
HEALTH, RELATIONSHIPS, AND CAREER.

I LIVE AN ABUNDANT LIFE.

I ATTRACT MONEY AND WEALTH THROUGH MY TALENTS
AND SKILLS.

I AM READY TO **SHARE MY GIFTS WITH THE WORLD.**

90

I RELEASE ALL FEARS AND ANXIETIES ABOUT MONEY.

I AM GRATEFUL FOR THE ABUNDANCE THAT I HAVE AND
THE ABUNDANCE THAT'S ON ITS WAY.

MY CREATIVITY BRINGS ME ABUNDANCE.

I ALWAYS **HAVE** ENOUGH **MONEY.**

I AM CAPABLE OF MANIFESTING ABUNDANCE THROUGH MY
THOUGHTS, WORDS, AND ACTIONS.

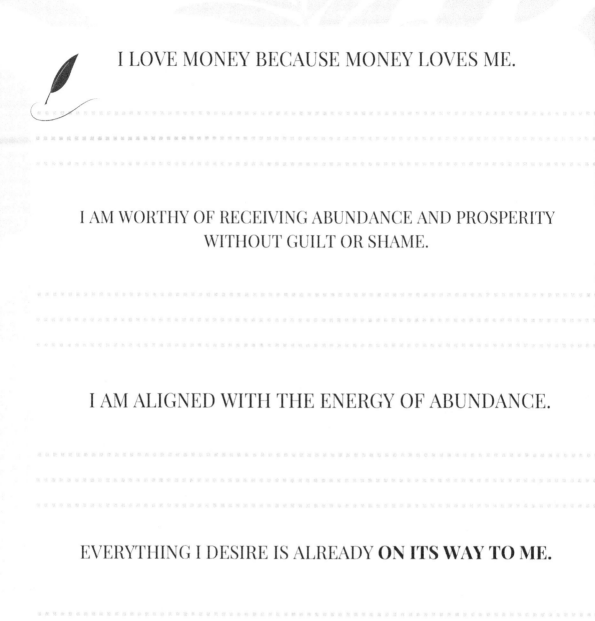

I LOVE MONEY BECAUSE MONEY LOVES ME.

I AM WORTHY OF RECEIVING ABUNDANCE AND PROSPERITY
WITHOUT GUILT OR SHAME.

I AM ALIGNED WITH THE ENERGY OF ABUNDANCE.

EVERYTHING I DESIRE IS ALREADY **ON ITS WAY TO ME.**

THE POWER OF **THE LAW OF ATTRACTION** BRINGS
ABUNDANCE INTO MY LIFE.

MORE AND MORE PROSPERITY FLOWS INTO MY LIFE.

I CHOOSE THE PATH OF WEALTH AND PROSPERITY
AND WALK IT EVERY DAY.

I FOCUS ON POSITIVITY AND **AM GRATEFUL** FOR ALL
THE ABUNDANCE I HAVE IN MY LIFE.

I AM WORTHY OF FINANCIAL FREEDOM AND
INDEPENDENCE, AND **I BELIEVE** THAT **I CAN** ACHIEVE IT.

I AM CAPABLE TO **CREATE MY REALITY** AND MANIFESTING
ABUNDANCE IN MY LIFE.

I MAKE SMART FINANCIAL DECISIONS AND INVEST IN
MY FUTURE.

I HAVE FULL TRUST IN MY AFFIRMATIONS FOR MONEY
ABUNDANCE.

I AM GROWING ABUNDANTLY EVERY DAY.

I AM GENEROUS AND THE UNIVERSE IS VERY
GENEROUS WITH ME.

I TRUST IN THE POWER OF GRATITUDE TO TRANSFORM
MY LIFE IN POSITIVE WAYS.

I AM SURROUNDED BY PEOPLE WHO SUPPORT AND UPLIFT
ME IN MY PURSUIT OF ABUNDANCE.

I AM PROUD OF THE **LIFE I AM BUILDING.**

I AM GRATEFUL FOR THE ABUNDANCE THAT **I AM BLESSED**
WITH EVERY DAY.

I AM A MAGNET FOR ABUNDANCE AND PROSPERITY.

I AM OPEN TO NEW OPPORTUNITIES AND ABUNDANCE THAT
COMES MY WAY.

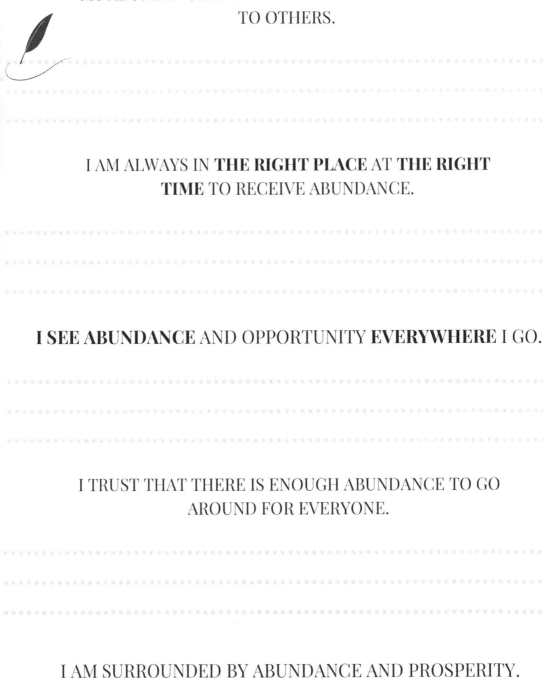

MY ABUNDANCE ENABLES ME TO GIVE GENEROUSLY
TO OTHERS.

I AM ALWAYS IN **THE RIGHT PLACE** AT **THE RIGHT
TIME** TO RECEIVE ABUNDANCE.

I SEE ABUNDANCE AND OPPORTUNITY **EVERYWHERE** I GO.

I TRUST THAT THERE IS ENOUGH ABUNDANCE TO GO
AROUND FOR EVERYONE.

I AM SURROUNDED BY ABUNDANCE AND PROSPERITY.

I ATTRACT ABUNDANCE BY FOCUSING ON WHAT I WANT,
NOT ON WHAT I LACK.

I AM ALIGNED WITH THE VIBRATION OF ABUNDANCE.

I AM AWARE OF **ABUNDANCE AROUND ME.**

I AM EXCITED TO SEE WHAT KIND OF ABUNDANCE IS
COMING MY WAY.

ABUNDANCE FLOWS TO ME EFFORTLESSLY AND EASILY.

I AM OPEN TO CREATIVE POSSIBILITIES FOR ABUNDANCE.

I AM GRATEFUL FOR ALL OF MY BLESSINGS.

I AM RECEIVING ABUNDANCE IN SO MANY WAYS.

I ATTRACT ABUNDANCE BY FOCUSING ON ABUNDANCE, NOT SCARCITY.

I TRUST IN **THE UNIVERSE** TO **PROVIDE ME WITH EVERYTHING I NEED** TO LIVE AN ABUNDANT LIFE.

I AM ABLE TO **SEE OPPORTUNITIES** FOR ABUNDANCE AND
WEALTH IN SITUATIONS AROUND ME.

ABUNDANCE IS A MINDSET, AND I CHOOSE TO
CULTIVATE IT DAILY.

I AM WORTHY TO RECEIVE THE FRUITS OF MY EFFORTS.

I AM FINANCIALLY **ABUNDANT AND SECURE.**

I CONTINUOUSLY MANIFEST ABUNDANCE.

 ABUNDANCE IS MY NATURAL STATE OF BEING.

I WELCOME ABUNDANCE **WITH** OPEN ARMS
AND AN **OPEN HEART.**

MY THOUGHTS AND ACTIONS ATTRACT
ABUNDANCE INTO MY LIFE.

I AM ALWAYS SUPPLIED WITH WHATEVER I NEED.

I AM PUTTING VALUE INTO THE WORLD, AND I
WILL BE REWARDED FOR IT.

"When you are grateful, fear disappears and abundance appears."
— Anthony Robbins

"When you realize there is nothing lacking, the whole world belongs to you."
-LAO TZU

"Abundance is not something we acquire. It is something we tune into."
-Wayne Dyer

"Abundance is about being rich, with or without money."
~ Suze Orman

"KEEP YOUR BEST WISHES, CLOSE TO YOUR HEART AND WATCH WHAT HAPPENS"
— TONY DELISO

"Why are you so enchanted by this world, when a mine of gold lies within you?"
~ Rumi

"Your fortune is not something to find but to unfold."
~ Eric Butterworth

"SEE YOURSELF LIVING IN ABUNDANCE AND YOU WILL ATTRACT IT, IT ALWAYS WORKS, IT WORKS EVERY TIME WITH EVERY PERSON." ~ BOB PROCTOR

"Abundance comes in many forms, do not limit your abundance by trying to control how it will flow, just know that it will come."
~ Shelly Sullivan

"PASSION IS THE PATH TO ABUNDANCE." - UNKNOWN

"I try to be grateful for the abundance of the blessings that I have, for the journey that I'm on and to relish each day as a gift."
~ James McGreevey

"Remember, no more effort is required to aim high in life, to demand abundance and prosperity than is required to accept misery and poverty."
~ Napoleon Hill

"WHEN YOU KEEP DOING WHAT YOU LOVE AND OPEN YOURSELF TO UNSEEN OPPORTUNITIES, THAT IS WHEN NATURE ALIGNS ITSELF TO BRING AN ABUNDANCE OF NEW THINGS FOR YOUR CREATION. DO WHAT YOU LOVE, AND LOVE WHAT YOU DO."
- ANAND PATWA

You are the author of your own story.
Take a deep breath and visualize a life filled with abundance and prosperity, where you have more than enough of everything you need. Write your affirmations with intention and purpose, knowing that you have the power to shape your future.

Success & Career

MY WILL IS STRONGER THAN ALL OBSTACLES.

I TRUST MY INTUITION TO GUIDE ME IN MAKING WISE CAREER DECISIONS.

I HAVE THE SKILLS AND KNOWLEDGE TO EXCEL IN MY PROFESSION.

I AM BUILDING A STRONG PERSONAL BRAND AND REPUTATION THAT REFLECTS MY VALUES, STRENGTHS AND ACHIEVEMENTS.

I AM GRATEFUL FOR THE OPPORTUNITIES THAT COME MY
WAY, AND I MAKE THE MOST OF THEM.

I AM A VALUABLE ASSET TO MY TEAM AND ORGANIZATION.

I BELIEVE IN MY UNIQUE TALENTS AND ABILITIES, AND I USE
THEM TO CREATE A POSITIVE IMPACT IN MY WORK.

I AM WILLING TO TAKE RISKS AND STEP OUTSIDE MY COMFORT
ZONE TO PURSUE MY DREAMS.

I AM CONSTANTLY EXPANDING MY NETWORK AND BUILDING
MEANINGFUL CONNECTIONS WITH COLLEAGUES AND
MENTORS.

I TRUST THE TIMING OF MY CAREER PROGRESSION AND
REMAIN PATIENT AND PERSISTENT IN **ACHIEVING MY GOALS.**

I HONOR MY VALUES AND ALIGN MY CAREER CHOICES
WITH MY PERSONAL AND PROFESSIONAL PRINCIPLES.

I AM FEARLESS IN TAKING CALCULATED RISKS TO PURSUE
MY PASSIONS AND ASPIRATIONS.

I CELEBRATE MY SUCCESSES AND LEARN FROM MY
FAILURES TO GROW AS A PROFESSIONAL.

I AM RESILIENT IN THE FACE OF CHALLENGES AND SETBACKS,
AND I BOUNCE BACK STRONGER THAN BEFORE.

I KNOW **I CAN ACHIEVE ANYTHING I WANT..**

I BALANCE MY CAREER WITH SELF–CARE AND
PRIORITIZE MY WELL–BEING.

I AM CREATIVE AND INNOVATIVE, AND I BRING FRESH
IDEAS AND PERSPECTIVES TO THE TABLE.

I KNOW A POSITIVE ATTITUDE CAN BRING ME SUCCESS.

MY CONFIDENCE AND SELF–BELIEF ARE MY BIGGEST
ASSETS TO **TAKE ME CLOSER TO MY SUCCESS.**

I AM A LEADER WHO INSPIRES AND EMPOWERS
OTHERS TO ACHIEVE THEIR BEST.

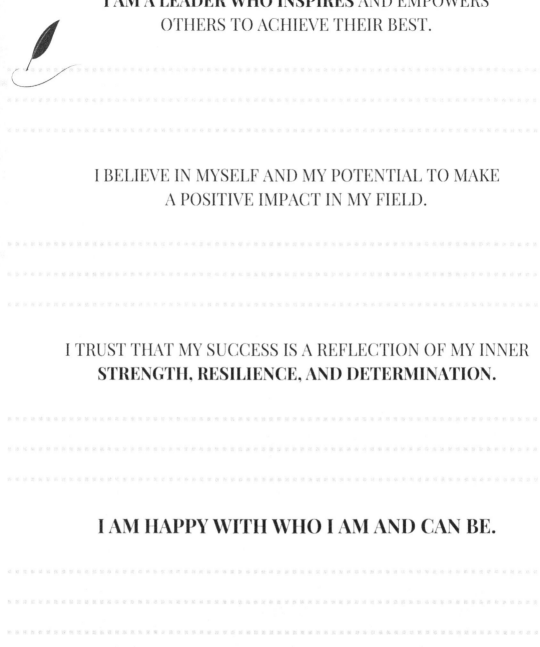

I BELIEVE IN MYSELF AND MY POTENTIAL TO MAKE
A POSITIVE IMPACT IN MY FIELD.

I TRUST THAT MY SUCCESS IS A REFLECTION OF MY INNER
STRENGTH, RESILIENCE, AND DETERMINATION.

I AM HAPPY WITH WHO I AM AND CAN BE.

I SET CLEAR AND REALISTIC PROFESSIONAL GOALS AND
MAKE ACTION PLANS TO ACHIEVE THEM.

I TRUST IN THE JOURNEY OF MY CAREER AND **REMAIN OPTIMISTIC** ABOUT THE OPPORTUNITIES AHEAD.

I AM A STRONG, CAPABLE, AND SUCCESSFUL WOMAN, AND I AM PROUD OF WHO I AM.

I AM WORTHY ENOUGH TO FOLLOW MY DREAMS AND MANIFEST MY DESIRES.

I AM HARDER THAN ALL THE CHALLENGES AND HURDLES LYING IN MY WAY.

I AM PREPARED FOR MY WILDEST DREAMS TO COME TRUE.

I AM BLESSED TO HAVE EVERYTHING IN MY LIFE TO
MAKE IT SUCCESSFUL.

I CONTINUE TO CLIMB HIGHER, **THERE ARE NO LIMITS** TO
WHAT I CAN ACHIEVE.

I AM A **TEAM PLAYER**, AND I COLLABORATE WITH OTHERS TO
ACHIEVE SHARED GOALS AND OBJECTIVES.

I LET GO OF OLD, NEGATIVE BELIEFS THAT HAVE
STOOD IN THE WAY OF MY SUCCESS.

THE WORLD NEEDS MY LIGHT AND I AM NOT
AFRAID TO SHINE.

I AM RESOURCEFUL, AND I FIND CREATIVE SOLUTIONS TO
PROBLEMS AND CHALLENGES.

I AM ALWAYS **OPEN-MINDED** AND EAGER TO EXPLORE NEW
AVENUES TO SUCCESS.

I STAY FOCUSED ON MY VISION AND PURSUE MY
DAILY WORK WITH PASSION.

I NEVER BACK DOWN UNDER PEER PRESSURE.

I AM A GOOD COMMUNICATOR, AND I EXPRESS MY IDEAS
AND OPINIONS WITH CLARITY AND CONFIDENCE.

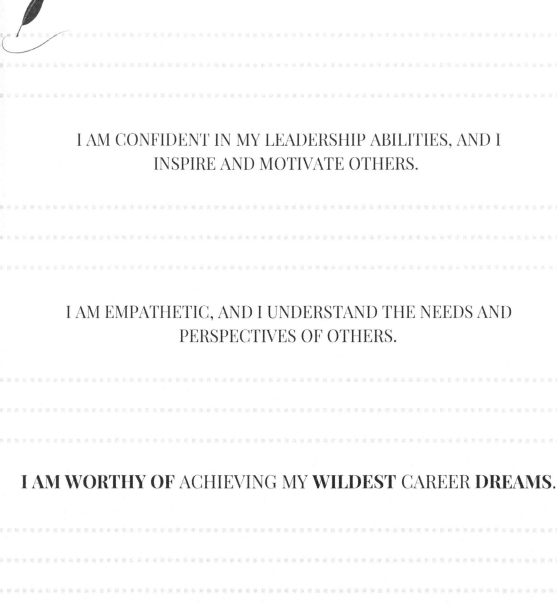

I AM DISCIPLINED, AND I STAY FOCUSED ON MY
PRIORITIES AND GOALS.

I AM CONFIDENT IN MY LEADERSHIP ABILITIES, AND I
INSPIRE AND MOTIVATE OTHERS.

I AM EMPATHETIC, AND I UNDERSTAND THE NEEDS AND
PERSPECTIVES OF OTHERS.

I AM WORTHY OF ACHIEVING MY **WILDEST** CAREER **DREAMS**.

I AM ORGANIZED, AND I MANAGE MY TIME AND RESOURCES
EFFICIENTLY AND EFFECTIVELY.

112

I AM RESPECTFUL, AND I TREAT OTHERS WITH KINDNESS
AND COMPASSION.

I TRUST THAT SUCCESS IS NOT **LIMITED** BY EXTERNAL
CIRCUMSTANCES, BUT **BY MY OWN MINDSET AND BELIEFS..**

I AM AUTHENTIC, AND **I STAY TRUE TO MYSELF** AND MY VALUES.

I HAVE THE POWER TO CREATE THE LIFE AND CAREER
OF MY DREAMS.

I MAKE THINGS HAPPEN AND I GET RESULTS.

I AM SELF-MOTIVATED, AND I TAKE OWNERSHIP OF MY CAREER AND MY SUCCESS.

I AM AMBITIOUS, AND I STRIVE TO REACH MY FULL POTENTIAL IN MY CAREER.

I GO ABOVE AND BEYOND TO ACHIEVE MY GOALS AND EXCEED EXPECTATIONS.

I AM CONSTANTLY IMPROVING AND **BECOMING MORE SUCCESSFUL** EVERY DAY.

I HAVE GOALS AND DREAMS THAT I AM GOING TO ACHIEVE.

I AM WORTHY OF ACHIEVING SUCCESS WITHOUT SACRIFICING MY
HEALTH, RELATIONSHIPS, OR HAPPINESS.

I AM A GOAL-GETTER AND WON'T STOP AT
ANYTHING TO ACHIEVE SUCCESS.

I BELIEVE THAT **I CAN DO ANYTHING.**

AS I BECOME MORE CONFIDENT IN MY ABILITY TO
SUCCEED, MORE DOORS OPEN FOR ME.

I KNOW THAT SUCCESS **IS POSSIBLE** FOR ME.

"Success is not achieved by winning all the time. Real success comes when we rise after we fall."
— Muhammad Ali

"Your positive action combined with positive thinking results in success."
-Shiv Khera

"Success is liking yourself, liking what you do, and liking how you do it."
— Maya Angelou

"LEARN AS IF YOU WILL LIVE FOREVER, LIVE LIKE YOU WILL DIE TOMORROW." – MAHATMA GANDHI

"Life is not measured by the number of breaths we take, but by the moments that take our breath away."
Maya Angelou.

"Success is not what you have, but who you are."
– Bo Bennett

"Success is not final; failure is not fatal: It is the courage to continue that counts."
— Winston S. Churchill

"Success is not something you pursue. Success is something you attract by the person you become."
– Jim Rohn

"Success is not about being the best. It's about always getting better."
-Behdad Sami

NEVER Give up!

"AMBITION IS THE PATH TO SUCCESS. PERSISTENCE IS THE VEHICLE YOU ARRIVE IN."
-BILL BRADLEY

"Success is not about being better than anyone else. It's about being better than you used to be."
– Wayne Dyer

The only limits are the ones you set for yourself. Close your eyes, take a deep breath, and believe in yourself and your abilities. Visualize your success. Write your affirmations with confidence and conviction, knowing that you can achieve anything you set your mind to.

Wealth

I AM FINANCIALLY FREE.

FINANCIAL WELL–BEING IS MY NEW REALITY.

MONEY FLOWS TO ME EASILY AND EFFORTLESSLY.

EVERYDAY **I AM BECOMING RICHER AND RICHER.**

MY MINDSET IS ALIGNED WITH WEALTH, AND I ATTRACT ABUNDANCE EFFORTLESSLY.

I AM CAPABLE OF CREATING WEALTH THROUGH MY CREATIVITY AND INNOVATION.

I AM CREATING A LIFE OF FINANCIAL FREEDOM AND ABUNDANCE.

I AM CAPABLE OF CREATING **MULTIPLE STREAMS OF INCOME** THAT SERVE MY PURPOSE AND PASSION.

I RELEASE ANY LIMITING BELIEFS ABOUT MONEY AND EMBRACE ABUNDANCE IN ALL FORMS.

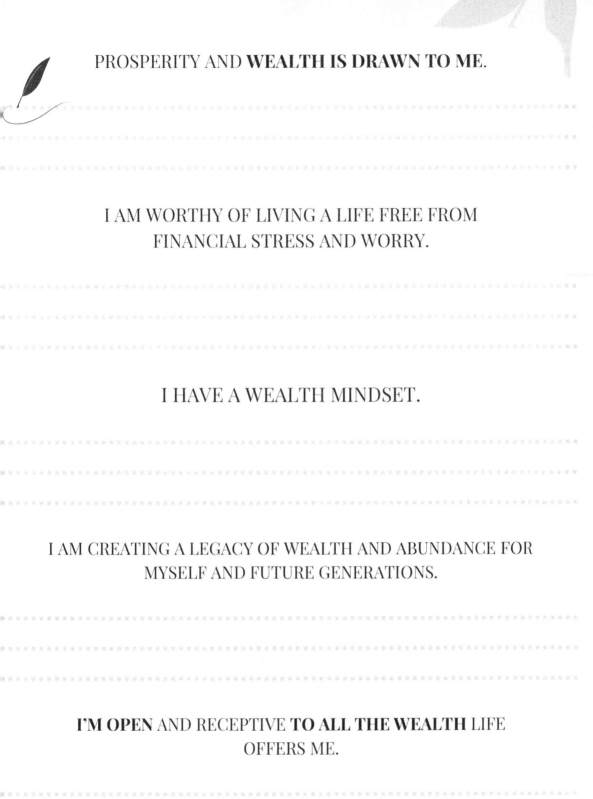

PROSPERITY AND **WEALTH IS DRAWN TO ME.**

I AM WORTHY OF LIVING A LIFE FREE FROM
FINANCIAL STRESS AND WORRY.

I HAVE A WEALTH MINDSET.

I AM CREATING A LEGACY OF WEALTH AND ABUNDANCE FOR
MYSELF AND FUTURE GENERATIONS.

I'M OPEN AND RECEPTIVE **TO ALL THE WEALTH** LIFE
OFFERS ME.

I AM WILLING TO GIVE GENEROUSLY AND SHARE MY WEALTH WITH OTHERS TO **CREATE POSITIVE CHANGE AND IMPACT.**

I AM MOTIVATED TO **TAKE ACTIONS** TOWARDS INCREASING MY INCOME AND BUILDING WEALTH.

I FEEL SO MARVELOUS AS A RICH PERSON.

LARGE **AMOUNTS OF MONEY ARE COMING TO ME** IN EVER INCREASING AMOUNTS.

I AM WORTHY OF RECEIVING AND ENJOYING THE FRUITS OF MY LABOR AND SUCCESS.

TODAY I AM ATTRACTING WEALTH, ABUNDANCE, AND WELLBEING.

I RELEASE EVERY BLOCK THAT HELD ME BACK FROM RECEIVING PROSPERITY.

MY LIFE IS RICH AND FULL.

I AM OPEN TO RECEIVING FINANCIAL ABUNDANCE **FROM UNEXPECTED SOURCES.**

MY FINANCIAL SUCCESS IS INEVITABLE.

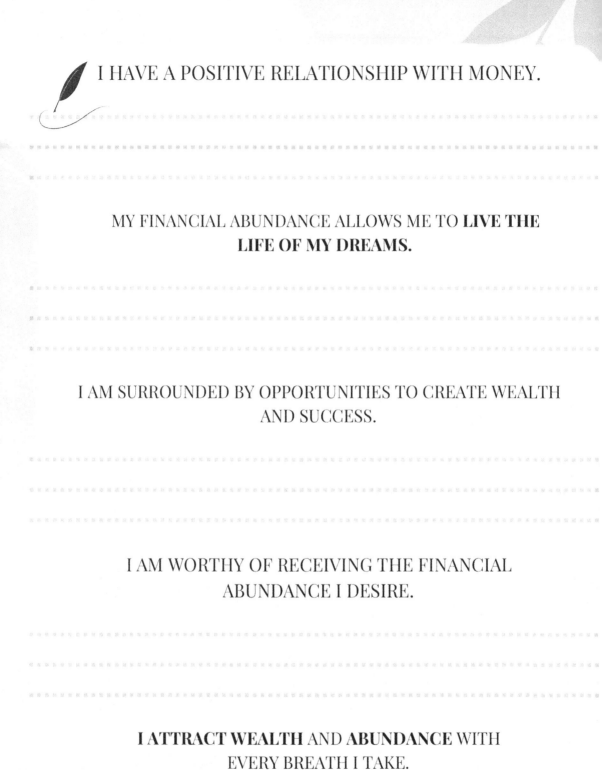

I HAVE A POSITIVE RELATIONSHIP WITH MONEY.

MY FINANCIAL ABUNDANCE ALLOWS ME TO **LIVE THE LIFE OF MY DREAMS.**

I AM SURROUNDED BY OPPORTUNITIES TO CREATE WEALTH AND SUCCESS.

I AM WORTHY OF RECEIVING THE FINANCIAL ABUNDANCE I DESIRE.

I ATTRACT WEALTH AND **ABUNDANCE** WITH EVERY BREATH I TAKE.

I TRUST THAT WEALTH AND ABUNDANCE ARE **POSSIBLE FOR ME,** AND I TAKE ACTION TOWARDS ACHIEVING IT.

I AM GRATEFUL FOR THE WEALTH THAT FLOWS INTO MY LIFE, AND I USE THEM WISELY TO CREATE MORE.

MY INCOME **EXCEEDS MY EXPECTATIONS.**

I AM GRATEFUL FOR THE FINANCIAL ABUNDANCE THAT SURROUNDS ME.

EVERY DAY IN EVERY WAY, I AM BECOMING MORE FINANCIALLY SUCCESSFUL.

THE UNIVERSE PROVIDES FOR ME ABUNDANTLY.

I AM FINANCIALLY SECURE AND STABLE.

I AM WORTHY OF HAVING EVERYTHING I DESIRE, INCLUDING FINANCIAL ABUNDANCE.

I AM COMMITTED TO CREATING WEALTH IN A WAY THAT IS ETHICAL AND **SERVES THE GREATER GOOD.**

FINANCIAL PROSPERITY COMES **NATURALLY** TO ME.

MY FINANCIAL SUCCESS **INCREASES** EVERY DAY.

I HAVE A POSITIVE MINDSET AROUND MONEY AND BELIEVE
THAT THERE IS ALWAYS ENOUGH TO GO AROUND.

MY BUSINESS GROWS AMAZINGLY EVERY DAY.

I KNOW THAT MY FINANCIAL SUCCESS IS ALIGNED WITH MY
HIGHEST GOOD AND THE GOOD OF OTHERS.

I AM GRATEFUL FOR MY ABILITY TO CREATE WEALTH
AND FINANCIAL SECURITY.

I AM A QUEEN OF MANAGING MY FINANCES.

MY FINANCES ARE HEALTHY AND THRIVING, AND **I AM GRATEFUL FOR THIS ABUNDANCE.**

RICHES FLOW THROUGH ME LIKE WAVES IN THE OCEAN AND COME BACK AGAIN.

I AM FREE FROM FINANCIAL **WORRIES** AND STRESS, AND I TRUST IN THE ABUNDANCE OF THE UNIVERSE.

I AM TAPPED INTO THE UNIVERSAL SUPPLY OF MONEY.

MY RICHES ARE FOREVER INCREASING AS I GIVE MORE OF
MYSELF IN SERVICE TO THE WORLD.

TODAY, NO MATTER WHERE I AM, **I FOCUS ON THAT
WHICH I WANT TO SEE.**

I MAKE SMART FINANCIAL DECISIONS THAT LEAD TO
LONG-TERM PROSPERITY.

I HAVE THE SKILLS AND KNOWLEDGE **TO MANAGE MONEY**
WISELY AND MAKE SMART FINANCIAL DECISIONS.

I AM ABUNDANT, RICH, WEALTHY, DESERVING, WORTHY.

THANKS TO THE MONEY I EARN, **I CAN FULFILL ALL MY DREAMS.**

I AM PROUD OF MY SUCCESS AND MY WEALTH.

I LIVE IN LUXURY AND PROSPERITY AND MONEY FLOWS
TO ME IN UNLIMITED AMOUNTS.

MY IMAGINATION HELPS ME MANIFEST WEALTH AND
LUXURY ON A CONSCIOUS AND UNCONSCIOUS LEVEL.

I AM A HEALTHY, WEALTHY AND SUCCESSFUL WOMAN.

"SEEK NOT GREATER WEALTH, BUT SIMPLER PLEASURE; NOT HIGHER FORTUNE, BUT DEEPER FELICITY."
— MAHATMA GHANDI

"Wealth is the ability to fully experience life."
- Henry David Thoreau

"Fortune sides with him who dares." –Virgil

"Success is not how many zeroes your bank account has. Its about making the most of the life you have."
- Suze Orman

"A wise person should have money in their head, but not in their heart."
–Jonathan Swift

"TOO MANY PEOPLE SPEND MONEY THEY EARNED TO BUY THINGS THEY DON'T WANT TO IMPRESS PEOPLE THAT THEY DON'T LIKE."
–WILL ROGERS

"The reason I've been able to be so financially successful is my focus has never, ever for one minute been money."
- Oprah Winfrey

"Being rich is not about how much money you have or how many homes you own; it's the freedom to buy any book you want without looking at the price and wondering if you can afford it."
— John Waters

"I'd rather have roses on my table than diamonds on my neck."
— Emma Goldman

"MONEY IS ONLY A TOOL. IT WILL TAKE YOU WHEREVER YOU WISH. BUT IT WILL NOT REPLACE YOU AS THE DRIVER." - AYN RAND

Don't blow off another's candle for it won't make yours shine brighter."
— Jaachynma N.E. Agu

"I would rather be able to appreciate things I cannot have than to have things I am not able to appreciate."
— Elbert Hubbard

"Wealth is the slave of a wise man. The master of a fool "
— Seneca,

Write down your affirmations that reflect your wealth mindset, and take consistent action towards your financial goals. Remember that wealth is more than just money, it is a mindset and a lifestyle, and you have the power to attract and create financial abundance by adopting a positive and proactive approach towards your finances.

Health & Well-being

MY BODY IS **STRONG, HEALTHY, AND RESILIENT.**

I AM COMMITTED TO **MAKING HEALTHY CHOICES** THAT
NOURISH MY BODY AND MIND.

I AM CAPABLE OF ACHIEVING **OPTIMAL HEALTH AND VITALITY,**
AND I TAKE ACTION TOWARD THIS GOAL EVERY DAY.

I LET GO OF HABITS AND BEHAVIORS THAT ARE HARMFUL TO
MY HEALTH AND REPLACE THEM WITH POSITIVE ONES.

I FOCUS ON THE POSITIVE AND LET GO OF STRESS AND
NEGATIVITY.

I PRIORITIZE SELF-CARE AND MAKE TIME FOR ACTIVITIES THAT
NOURISH MY MIND, BODY, AND SOUL.

MY MIND AND BODY ARE IN **PERFECT HARMONY AND BALANCE.**

I AM GRATEFUL FOR EACH DAY THAT I AM HEALTHY
AND STRONG.

I AM COMMITTED TO EDUCATING MYSELF ABOUT HEALTH
AND WELLNESS.

I CHOOSE TO FOCUS ON **PROGRESS RATHER THAN PERFECTION** AND CELEBRATE EVERY SMALL STEP TOWARD BETTER HEALTH.

I LISTEN TO THE INTUITION I HAVE ABOUT MY HEALING.

I AM WORTHY OF A LIFE FULL OF VITALITY AND ENERGY, AND EVERY DAY I TAKE STEPS TOWARD THAT GOAL.

I AM STRONG, HEALTHY, AND FULL OF ENERGY.

I CHOOSE TO HONOR AND CHERISH MY HEALTH EVERY DAY.

I MAKE CHOICES THAT SUPPORT MY WELL-BEING.

I AM GRATEFUL FOR MY BODY AND ALL THAT IT DOES FOR
ME, AND I TREAT IT WITH LOVE AND RESPECT.

MY MENTAL HEALTH IS AT AN **EXCELLENT LEVEL.**

I TRUST IN THE WISDOM OF MY BODY AND **LISTEN TO
ITS NEEDS AND SIGNALS.**

EVERY DAY, MY BODY AND MIND BECOME STRONGER
AND MORE RESILIENT.

I AM CAPABLE OF MANAGING STRESS AND FINDING
BALANCE IN MY LIFE.

I AM GRATEFUL FOR THE HEALING POWER OF NATURE, AND
I TAKE TIME TO CONNECT WITH THE NATURAL WORLD.

I NOURISH MY BODY WITH HEALTHY FOODS AND
ACTIVITIES.

I AM GRATEFUL AND **HAPPY TO BE ALIVE.**

I TRUST IN THE HEALING POWER OF MY BODY AND MIND.

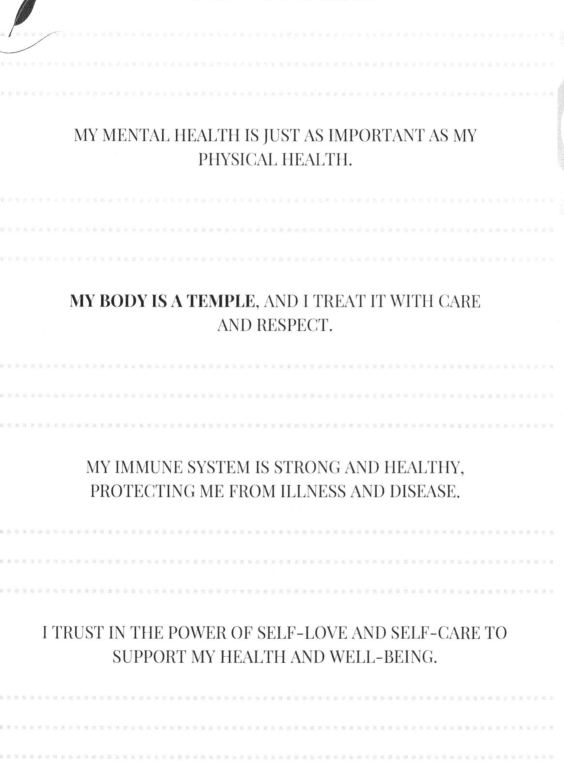

EVERY BREATH I TAKE FILLS ME WITH
VITALITY AND **ENERGY.**

MY MENTAL HEALTH IS JUST AS IMPORTANT AS MY
PHYSICAL HEALTH.

MY BODY IS A TEMPLE, AND I TREAT IT WITH CARE
AND RESPECT.

MY IMMUNE SYSTEM IS STRONG AND HEALTHY,
PROTECTING ME FROM ILLNESS AND DISEASE.

I TRUST IN THE POWER OF SELF-LOVE AND SELF-CARE TO
SUPPORT MY HEALTH AND WELL-BEING.

MY BODY KNOWS HOW TO **HEAL ITSELF**.

I MAKE HEALTHY CHOICES THAT SUPPORT MY PHYSICAL,
MENTAL, AND EMOTIONAL WELL-BEING.

I AM DETERMINED TO **CURE MY WOUNDS, SOUL,
MIND,** AND SEE THINGS DIFFERENTLY.

I AM SURROUNDED BY PEOPLE WHO **SUPPORT** MY JOURNEY
TOWARDS HEALTH AND WELLNESS.

MY MIND IS AT PEACE.

MY MIND IS POWERFUL AND I USE IT TO CREATE POSITIVE CHANGES IN MY LIFE.

I RELEASE ALL NEGATIVE THOUGHTS AND EMOTIONS, ALLOWING MY MIND AND BODY TO HEAL.

I AM IN CONTROL OF MY THOUGHTS AND ACTIONS AND CHOOSE HEALTHY AND POSITIVE BEHAVIORS.

MY WELLNESS IS A **PRIORITY** TO ME.

I AM HAPPY AND FULFILLED IN MY PURSUIT OF A HEALTHY AND BALANCED LIFESTYLE.

I CHOOSE TO LET GO OF UNHEALTHY HABITS AND BELIEFS
THAT NO LONGER SERVE ME.

I AM HAPPY, HEALTHY, AND WHOLE, AND MY VIBRANT
HEALTH RADIATES OUT INTO THE WORLD AROUND ME.

I AM GRATEFUL FOR MY BODY'S ABILITY TO HEAL AND
REGENERATE.

MY SLEEP IS RELAXED AND REFRESHING.

EVERY DAY, IN EVERY WAY, I AM BECOMING
BETTER AND BETTER.

I AM THANKFUL FOR EVERYTHING MY BODY PROVIDES.

I AM GRATEFUL FOR THE HEALTH AND VITALITY THAT
I ALREADY HAVE IN MY LIFE.

MY BODY AND MIND LISTEN TO ME.

I TRUST THAT MY BODY HAS THE INNATE ABILITY
TO HEAL ITSELF.

I AM WORTHY OF EXPERIENCING A **LIFE FREE FROM
CHRONIC ILLNESS AND PAIN.**

I AM GRATEFUL FOR THE CHALLENGES IN MY LIFE THAT HAVE HELPED ME GROW AND APPRECIATE MY HEALTH EVEN MORE.

THERE IS HOPE, CONFIDENCE, AND **VIGOR**
ALL AROUND ME.

I AM GRATEFUL FOR THE **SIMPLE PLEASURES** IN LIFE THAT
BRING ME JOY AND NOURISH MY BODY AND MIND.

I MEDITATE TO FREE MY MIND FROM ILL THOUGHTS.

MY BODY LOVES AND PROTECTS ME.

I TAKE TIME TO RELAX AND RECHARGE MY MIND
AND BODY.

I HAVE RECEIVED THE BLESSING OF HEALTH
AND WELL-BEING.

I TAKE TIME TO REFLECT AND CONNECT WITH MY
INNER SELF.

I AM GRATEFUL FOR THE OPPORTUNITIES THAT BRING ME
CLOSER TO OPTIMAL HEALTH AND WELL-BEING.

MY IMMUNE SYSTEM IS STRONG AND PROTECTS ME
FROM ILLNESS.

"TO ENSURE GOOD HEALTH: EAT LIGHTLY, BREATHE DEEPLY, LIVE MODERATELY, CULTIVATE CHEERFULNESS, AND MAINTAIN AN INTEREST IN LIFE." – WILLIAM LONDEN

"A healthy outside starts from the inside. – Robert Urich

"Health is a state of complete harmony of the body, mind, and spirit." – B.K.S. Iyengar

"Your body hears everything your mind says." – Naomi Judd

"I have chosen to be happy because it is good for my health." - Voltaire

"A good laugh and a long sleep are the best cures in the doctor's book." – Irish proverb

"The wish for healing has always been half of health." – Lucius Annaeus Seneca

"It is health which is real wealth and not pieces of gold and silver." – Mahatma Gandhi

'TAKE CARE OF YOUR BODY. IT'S THE ONLY PLACE YOU HAVE TO LIVE IN.' – JIM ROHN

"WRITE DOWN THE THINGS THAT ARE ON YOUR MIND. THE SIMPLE ACT OF LISTING YOUR THOUGHTS CAN HAVE A CATHARTIC AND HEALING EFFECT." – JULIA LAFLIN

"A SAD SOUL CAN BE JUST AS LETHAL AS A GERM." – JOHN STEINBECK

"Values are related to our emotions, just as we practice physical hygiene to preserve our physical health, we need to observe emotional hygiene to preserve a healthy mind and attitudes." – Dalai Lama

"We are what we repeatedly do. Excellence, then, is not an act, but a habit." – Will Durant

"Time and health are two precious assets that we don't recognize and appreciate until they have been depleted." – Denis Waitley

146

Begin by prioritizing your physical, mental, and emotional health as a top priority in your life. Manifest your health and well-being. Write your affirmations with enthusiasm and excitement, knowing that your potential is limitless. You are capable of amazing things.

Positive Thinking

I CHOOSE TO FOCUS ON **POSITIVE THOUGHTS AND FEELINGS** EVERY DAY.

POSITIVE THINKING COMES NATURALLY TO ME.

I CHOOSE TO LET GO OF NEGATIVE THOUGHTS AND REPLACE THEM WITH POSITIVE ONES.

I ATTRACT POSITIVE PEOPLE AND EXPERIENCES INTO MY LIFE.

I AM GRATEFUL FOR ALL THE POSITIVE
EXPERIENCES IN MY LIFE.

POSITIVE THINKING EMPOWERS ME TO TAKE ACTION
TOWARDS MY GOALS AND DREAMS.

I CHOOSE TO **FOCUS ON SOLUTIONS** RATHER
THAN PROBLEMS.

I SEE THE POTENTIAL FOR GROWTH AND POSITIVE
CHANGE IN EVERY SITUATION.

I BELIEVE IN MYSELF AND MY ABILITY TO CREATE A
POSITIVE AND FULFILLING LIFE.

I CHOOSE TO FOCUS ON MY STRENGTHS AND ACCOMPLISHMENTS
RATHER THAN MY WEAKNESSES AND FAILURES.

POSITIVE THINKING HELPS ME TO SEE OPPORTUNITIES
WHERE OTHERS SEE OBSTACLES.

I AM CONSTANTLY GROWING AND EVOLVING THROUGH
POSITIVE THINKING AND SELF-REFLECTION.

I ALWAYS HAVE **A POSITIVE STATE OF MIND.**

I AM FILLED WITH POSITIVITY AND LIGHT, AND I SHARE
THAT ENERGY WITH EVERYONE I MEET.

I AM CAPABLE OF CREATING A POSITIVE AND
FULFILLING LIFE.

I SEE **THE GLASS AS HALF FULL**, NEVER AS HALF EMPTY.

I SEE THE GOOD IN EVERY SITUATION AND FIND
OPPORTUNITIES FOR GROWTH AND LEARNING.

I AM GRATEFUL FOR ALL THE GOOD THINGS IN MY LIFE.

POSITIVE THINKING IS A HABIT THAT I CULTIVATE DAILY.

I APPROACH EVERY SITUATION WITH A POSITIVE AND
OPTIMISTIC MINDSET.

I CHOOSE TO **SEE THE BEST IN MYSELF** AND OTHERS.

I AM GRATEFUL FOR THE GIFT OF LIFE AND ALL
ITS BLESSINGS.

I AM FEELING POSITIVE, HEALTHY AND STRONG TODAY.

MY THOUGHTS CREATE MY REALITY, AND I CHOOSE TO THINK
POSITIVELY.

I BANISH ALL SELF-DOUBT FROM MY MIND AND I EMBRACE
HOPE, OPTIMISM AND COMPASSION.

I AM SURROUNDED BY PEOPLE WHO UPLIFT AND INSPIRE
ME TO THINK POSITIVELY.

I CHOOSE TO **SEE THE BRIGHT SIDE** OF EVERY SITUATION.

I CHOOSE TO SEE THE BEAUTY IN THE WORLD AROUND ME AND
APPRECIATE THE SIMPLE THINGS IN LIFE.

I TRUST IN THE PROCESS OF LIFE AND KNOW THAT
EVERYTHING IS HAPPENING FOR MY HIGHEST GOOD.

I AM CAPABLE OF CONTROLLING MY THOUGHTS AND **CHOOSING POSITIVITY** OVER NEGATIVITY.

TO MAKE **SMALL STEPS** TOWARDS BIG GOALS, **IS PROGRESS.**

THERE IS NO GREATER GOAL THAN BEING CONTENT WITH YOURSELF.

I AM LETTING GO OF LIMITING BELIEFS AND NEGATIVE SELF-TALK THAT HOLD ME BACK FROM LIVING MY BEST LIFE.

I CELEBRATE MY SUCCESSES AND ACHIEVEMENTS AND USE THEM TO FUEL MY POSITIVITY.

I TRUST IN **THE POWER OF VISUALIZATION** TO MANIFEST MY DESIRES AND DREAMS INTO **REALITY**.

NO NEGATIVE THOUGHT WILL TAKE ROOT IN MY MIND.

I ENJOY THE PRESENT MOMENT AND APPRECIATE THE LITTLE THINGS IN LIFE.

I CREATE POSITIVE RELATIONSHIPS WITH OTHERS THROUGH KINDNESS, EMPATHY AND UNDERSTANDING.

I USE POSITIVE AFFIRMATIONS AND SELF-TALK TO BOOST MY CONFIDENCE AND SELF-ESTEEM.

I HAVE A **POSITIVE IMPACT** ON SOMEONE'S LIFE.

I BELIEVE THAT I CAN INSPIRE AND MOTIVATE OTHERS
WITH MY POSITIVE ATTITUDE AND ENERGY.

I AM THANKFUL FOR WHAT I HAVE, EVEN IF IT IS NOT PERFECT.

EVERY DAY **I KEEP MY MIND AND HEART OPEN.**

MY GREATEST STRUGGLES, ARE MY GREATEST LESSONS.

I'M RISING ABOVE THE THOUGHTS THAT ARE TRYING
TO MAKE ME ANGRY OR AFRAID.

I TURN DOWN THE VOLUME OF NEGATIVITY IN MY LIFE,
WHILE TURNING UP THE VOLUME OF THE POSITIVE.

I EXPERIENCE POSITIVE EMOTIONS SUCH AS **LOVE, GRATITUDE,
AND HAPPINESS** ON A DAILY BASIS.

I AM NOT PUSHED BY MY PROBLEMS; **I AM LED
BY MY DREAMS.**

I CHOOSE TO SPREAD POSITIVITY AND LOVE WHEREVER I GO.

I LET GO OF FEAR AND **EMBRACE THE UNKNOWN** WITH EXCITEMENT AND ANTICIPATION.

I CAN BE WHATEVER I WANT TO BE.

I KNOW THAT ONE **SMALL POSITIVE THOUGHT** IN THE MORNING **CAN CHANGE MY WHOLE DAY.**

I AM WORTHY OF LIVING A LIFE FILLED WITH POSITIVE ENERGY, MOTIVATION, AND INSPIRATION.

LIFE IS GETTING BETTER ALL THE TIME!

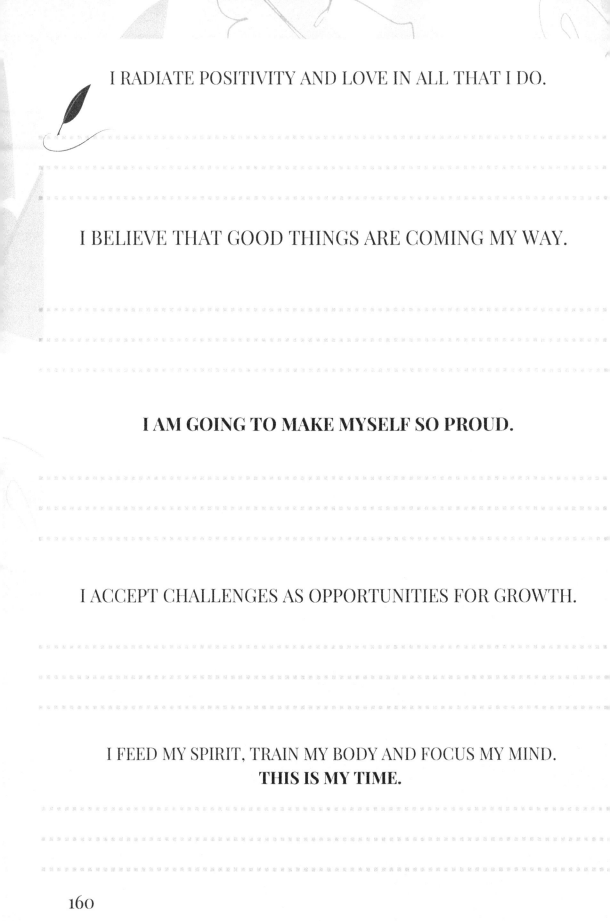

I RADIATE POSITIVITY AND LOVE IN ALL THAT I DO.

I BELIEVE THAT GOOD THINGS ARE COMING MY WAY.

I AM GOING TO MAKE MYSELF SO PROUD.

I ACCEPT CHALLENGES AS OPPORTUNITIES FOR GROWTH.

I FEED MY SPIRIT, TRAIN MY BODY AND FOCUS MY MIND.
THIS IS MY TIME.

"POSITIVE THINKING IS NOT A GUARANTEE OF SUCCESS, BUT IT CERTAINLY MAKES IT MORE LIKELY."
- EARL NIGHTINGALE

"Great things happen to those who don't stop believing, trying, learning, and being grateful." — Roy T. Bennett

"Positive thinking is not about ignoring life's problems, it's about understanding that challenges are opportunities to learn and grow." - Robin Sharma

"You only live once, but if you do it right, once is enough."
— Mae West

"Positive thinking is the foundation of a happy and successful life. It allows us to see opportunities instead of obstacles, solutions instead of problems, and blessings instead of burdens." - Michael Josephson

"try to be a rainbow in someone else's cloud."
— Maya Angelou

"Positive thinking is contagious. People who think positively are more likely to attract positive energy and people into their lives." -Unknown

"Once you replace negative thoughts with positive ones, you'll start having positive results." – Willie Nelson

"SOMETIMES, WHEN THINGS ARE FALLING APART, THEY MAY ACTUALLY BE FALLING INTO PLACE."
— UNKNOWN

"The greatest discovery of my generation is that a human being can alter his life by altering his attitudes." - William James

"CHOOSE TO BE OPTIMISTIC, IT FEELS BETTER."
— Dali Lama

"the positive thinker sees the invisible, feels the intangible, and achieves the impossible."
- Winston Churchill

"Perpetual optimism is a force multiplier." — Colin Powell

"Positive thinking is a powerful force that can transform your life and help you achieve your dreams."
- Les Brown

"The mind is everything. What you think you become." - Buddha

Focus on the positive aspects of your life and the world around you, even if they may seem small. Every day is a new opportunity to make progress toward your goals. Write your affirmations with gratitude and optimism, knowing that good things are coming your way.

Motivation

I AM HIGHLY MOTIVATED AND FOCUSED ON
ACHIEVING MY GOALS.

I AM CAPABLE OF ACHIEVING ANYTHING I SET MY MIND TO.

MY MOTIVATION COMES FROM WITHIN, AND
IT **IS UNSHAKEABLE.**

I AM MOTIVATED BY MY DESIRE TO **MAKE A POSITIVE IMPACT** IN
THE WORLD.

I AM FILLED WITH ENTHUSIASM AND EXCITEMENT FOR THE
OPPORTUNITIES THAT LIE AHEAD.

A SYNONYM FOR THE WORD **DREAMS** IS THEIR **REALIZATION**.

I SET MY GOALS HIGH AND WORK HARD EVERY
DAY TO REACH THEM.

THE TIME HAS COME TO CREATE THE LIFE I CHOOSE.

MY PAST MIGHT BE UGLY, BUT I AM STILL BEAUTIFUL.

I AM A LIVING, BREATHING EXAMPLE OF MOTIVATION.

I AM RESILIENT AND PERSISTENT, AND I BOUNCE BACK QUICKLY
FROM SETBACKS AND FAILURES.

EVERY DAY, **I AM TAKING STEPS** TOWARDS
ACHIEVING MY DREAMS.

THE ONLY LIMITS ARE THE ONES I IMPOSE ON MYSELF.

EVEN WHEN IT HURTS, I ATTACK MY GOALS MORE INTENSELY.

EVERY DAY I WAKE UP WITH A RENEWED SENSE OF
PURPOSE AND DETERMINATION.

I AM DRIVEN TO SUCCEED AND OVERCOME ANY
OBSTACLES THAT COME MY WAY.

I AM CONSTANTLY PUSHING MYSELF TO BE **THE BEST
VERSION OF MYSELF.**

I AM PASSIONATE ABOUT MY WORK AND **FIND JOY** IN
EVERY TASK I UNDERTAKE.

I AM **DETERMINED** TO TURN MY DREAMS INTO REALITY.

I VISUALIZE MY GOALS DAILY AND FEEL THE JOY OF
ACCOMPLISHING THEM.

I AM MOTIVATED BY MY VISION FOR THE FUTURE, AND I WORK
TIRELESSLY TO BRING IT TO FRUITION.

I CONCENTRATE ALL MY EFFORTS ON THE THINGS I
WANT TO ACCOMPLISH IN LIFE.

FAILURE IS JUST THE SPRINGBOARD OF A STRING OF SUCCESSES.

I AM DRIVEN TO SUCCEED BECAUSE I KNOW THAT MY SUCCESS
WILL INSPIRE OTHERS TO DO THE SAME.

SUCCESS TAKES TIME AND PATIENCE – I AM PERSISTENT.

THE WORD FATIGUE IS AN ILLUSION, I CONTINUE TO PUSH
FORWARD TO MY INTENDED GOALS.

I ACT WITH **COURAGE** AND CONFIDENCE.

I KEEP GOING, ONE STEP AT A TIME, MY HARD
WORK WILL PAY OFF.

MY DREAMS ARE IMPORTANT AND WORTH PURSUING.

I AM FILLED WITH POSITIVE ENERGY AND VITALITY, AND I MAKE
THE MOST OF EVERY MOMENT.

I HAVE A **CLEAR VISION OF WHAT I WANT TO ACHIEVE,**
AND I TAKE STEPS TOWARDS IT EVERY DAY.

I AM MOTIVATED BY THE LOVE AND SUPPORT OF THOSE WHO
BELIEVE IN ME AND MY VISION.

I WILL LIVE MY LIFE AS THE EXCITING
ADVENTURE THAT IT IS.

I LIVE IN THE PRESENT, NEVER DWELLING ON THE PAST, AND
TAKE ACTION TO ENSURE A WONDERFUL FUTURE.

I AM THE ONLY ONE RESPONSIBLE FOR GIVING
MYSELF THE LIFE I WANT.

I AM DISCIPLINED AND TAKE CONSISTENT **ACTION
TOWARDS MY GOALS.**

I TAKE BOLD AND DARING LEAPS.

ANYTHING IS POSSIBLE IF I BELIEVE I CAN DO IT.

I CELEBRATE MY SMALL VICTORIES ON THE WAY
TO ACHIEVING MY GOALS.

I AM FLEXIBLE AND WILLING TO ADJUST MY PLANS TO
ACHIEVE MY GOALS.

EVERY **SMALL STEP** I TAKE MAKES A **BIG DIFFERENCE**.

I AM MOTIVATED BY THE **SATISFACTION** AND JOY THAT COMES
FROM MAKING PROGRESS TOWARDS MY GOALS.

I AM WORTHY OF TAKING BREAKS AND REST TO RECHARGE MY
ENERGY AND MOTIVATION.

I MAY MAKE MISTAKES, BUT **I DON'T QUIT**.

I AM MOTIVATED TO **PURSUE MY PASSIONS**
AND PURPOSE IN LIFE.

I COURAGEOUSLY WALK THROUGH EVERY DOOR
OF OPPORTUNITY.

I AM MORE THAN ENOUGH.

I AM CAPABLE OF PUSHING THROUGH SELF-DOUBT
AND FEAR TO ACHIEVE GREATNESS.

I CAN SUCCEED. **I WILL SUCCEED.**

I MAKE MY OWN MAGIC.

NOTHING CAN STOP ME FROM GETTING THINGS DONE.

I CAN AND I WILL. I BELIEVE IN ME.

I CLEARLY VISUALIZE HOW I FEEL WHEN I ACHIEVE MY GOALS.

I HAVE FAITH IN MYSELF AND DO NOT GIVE UP,
GREAT THINGS ARE WAITING FOR ME.

I TURN MY DREAMS INTO GOALS, MY GOALS INTO PLANS, AND MY PLANS **INTO REALITY.**

I HAVE WHAT IT TAKES TO BE SUCCESSFUL IN ALL THAT I DO.

I AM LIVING MY BEST LIFE RIGHT NOW!

I AM ALIGNING MY PRIORITIES AND TAKING LIFE TO THE NEXT LEVEL.

I AM INCREDIBLY STRONG AND DETERMINED AND HAVE BOUNDLESS FAITH IN MYSELF.

"Motivation is what gets you started. Habit is what keeps you going."

- Jim Ryun

"the only way to do great work is to love what you do. If you haven't found it yet, keep looking. Don't settle. As with all matters of the heart, you'll know when you find it."
- Steve Jobs

"Don't watch the clock; do what it does. Keep going."
- Sam Levenson

"You can't build a reputation on what you are going to do."
- Henry Ford

"I AM THE GREATEST. I SAID THAT EVEN BEFORE I KNEW I WAS." - MUHAMMAD ALI

"STAY AWAY FROM THOSE PEOPLE WHO TRY TO DISPARAGE YOUR AMBITIONS. SMALL MINDS WILL ALWAYS DO THAT, BUT GREAT MINDS WILL GIVE YOU A FEELING THAT YOU CAN BECOME GREAT TOO." - MARK TWAIN

"The way to get started is to quit talking and begin doing." - Walt Disney

"LIFE IS LIKE A BICYCLE. TO KEEP YOUR BALANCE, YOU MUST KEEP MOVING."
– ALBERT EINSTEIN

"The greatest glory in living lies not in never falling, but in rising every time we fall."
- Nelson Mandela

"Nothing is impossible, the word itself says 'I'm possible.'"
— Audrey Hepburn

"Believe you can and you're halfway there."
- Theodore Roosevelt

"It does not matter how slowly you go as long as you do not stop."
- Confucius

"You are never too old to set another goal or to dream a new dream." - C.S. Lewis

"I have not failed. I've just found 10,000 ways that won't work."
– Thomas Edison

"You miss 100% of the shots you don't take."
- Wayne Gretzky

"I CAN'T CHANGE THE DIRECTION OF THE WIND, BUT I CAN ADJUST MY SAILS TO ALWAYS REACH MY DESTINATION."
- JIMMY DEAN

176

Don't be afraid to dream big! Close your eyes and visualize a life where you are motivated and driven to pursue your passions and achieve your dreams. Write your affirmations with confidence and determination, knowing that you have what it takes to make them a reality.

Intuition

MY HIGHEST SELF GUIDES MY ACTIONS AND DECISIONS.

I AM CONNECTED TO MY INNER WISDOM AND TRUST MY INTUITION TO GUIDE ME.

I BELIEVE THE UNIVERSE WILL PROVIDE ME WITH THE ANSWERS I NEED.

I TRUST IN THE MESSAGES THAT COME TO ME THROUGH MY INTUITION.

I TRUST MY INNER WISDOM TO GUIDE ME TO THE RIGHT
PEOPLE, PLACES AND EXPERIENCES.

I AM GRATEFUL FOR MY INTUITION AND THE GUIDANCE IT
PROVIDES ME.

I HONOR THE SACRED DIVINITY THAT EXISTS WITHIN ME.

I AM CONSTANTLY GROWING AND EXPANDING MY INTUITION
THROUGH **MEDITATION, REFLECTION, AND SELF-CARE.**

MY INTUITION HELPS ME TO STAY ALIGNED WITH MY SOUL'S
PURPOSE AND HIGHEST POTENTIAL.

I AM INSIGHTFUL, INTUITIVE, AND IMAGINATIVE.

MY INNER KNOWING ALWAYS **KNOWS THE WAY.**

I AM ALIGNED WITH THE LOVING WILL OF THE UNIVERSE.

I TRUST **THE PULL IN MY HEART** TO GUIDE ME FORWARD.

I HEAR, SEE AND KNOW THE TRUTH ABOUT ALL THINGS.

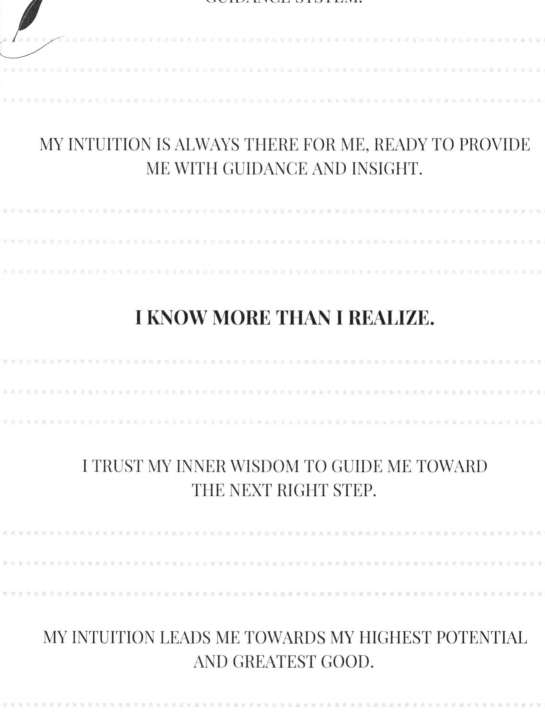

I RELEASE ALL BLOCKAGES THAT OBSCURE MY INNER
GUIDANCE SYSTEM.

MY INTUITION IS ALWAYS THERE FOR ME, READY TO PROVIDE
ME WITH GUIDANCE AND INSIGHT.

I KNOW MORE THAN I REALIZE.

I TRUST MY INNER WISDOM TO GUIDE ME TOWARD
THE NEXT RIGHT STEP.

MY INTUITION LEADS ME TOWARDS MY HIGHEST POTENTIAL
AND GREATEST GOOD.

I AM CONNECTED WITH MY HIGHER SELF AND
SPIRITUAL GUIDANCE.

I RECEIVE INTUITIVE MESSAGES FROM THE UNIVERSE.

I TRUST IN THE SIGNS AND SYNCHRONICITIES THAT
COME TO ME.

MY INNER GUIDE IS DEEP, PROFOUND, AND IMMEASURABLE.

I KNOW THE NEXT RIGHT STEP BECAUSE **I FEEL IT
IN MY HEART.**

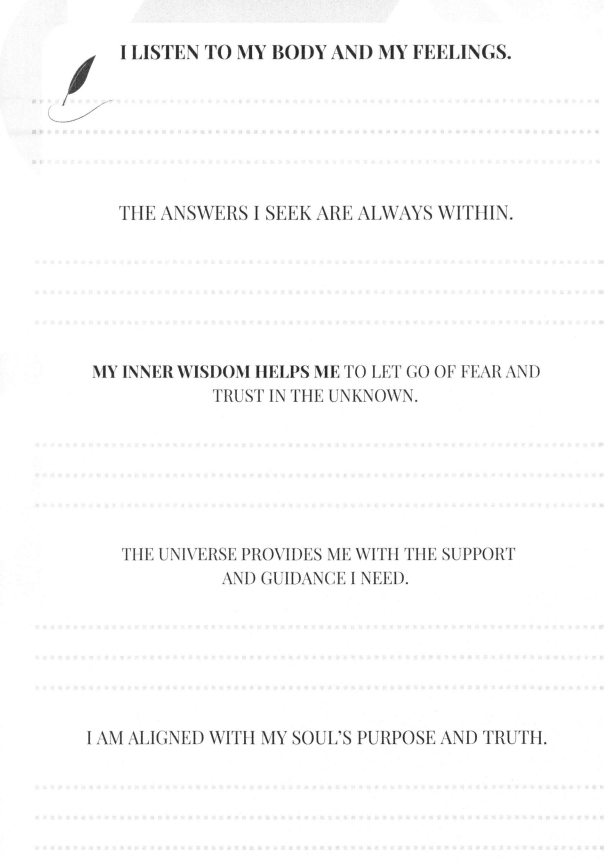

I LISTEN TO MY BODY AND MY FEELINGS.

THE ANSWERS I SEEK ARE ALWAYS WITHIN.

MY INNER WISDOM HELPS ME TO LET GO OF FEAR AND
TRUST IN THE UNKNOWN.

THE UNIVERSE PROVIDES ME WITH THE SUPPORT
AND GUIDANCE I NEED.

I AM ALIGNED WITH MY SOUL'S PURPOSE AND TRUTH.

MY INNER WISDOM IS ALWAYS WORKING IN MY BEST
INTEREST AND HIGHEST GOOD.

I DEEPEN **MY CONNECTION WITH THE DIVINE** AND
DISCOVER THE UNIQUE WAYS IN WHICH IT SPEAKS TO
ME.

I OPEN MYSELF TO SEEING NEW POSSIBILITIES THAT
ALIGN WITH MY SPIRIT.

I FEEL THE WISDOM OF ALL OF LIFE EMBEDDED WITHIN
MY BODY MIND AND SPIRIT.

I AM THE SOURCE OF MY TRUTH.

I AM OPEN TO RECEIVING INTUITIVE GUIDANCE AND
INSIGHTS FROM UNEXPECTED SOURCES.

I LIVE IN ALIGNMENT WITH **MY AUTHENTIC SELF.**

I TRUST AND HONOR MY INTUITION AS A VALUABLE AND
ESSENTIAL PART OF MYSELF.

WHENEVER I AM IN DOUBT, I ALWAYS LISTEN TO MY INTUITION.

EVERY DAY I TRUST MY HUNCHES MORE AND MORE.

EVERYTHING I NEED IS WITHIN ME.

IF I QUIET MY MIND, THE ANSWERS WILL COME TO ME.

I AM GRATEFUL FOR THE PEACE AND CLARITY THAT MY
INTUITION BRINGS INTO MY LIFE.

MY INTUITION KNOWS THE WAY.

I OPEN MYSELF TO KNOW MY INNER GUIDANCE AND
DEEPEST WISDOM.

I USE MY INTUITION AND INSIGHT WITHOUT FEAR OR DELUSION.

I AM A LOVING SOUL IN A HUMAN BODY.

I AM STEPPING INTO A NEW AND FRESH **AWARENESS**.

I AM A DIVINE BEING AND I AM IN CONNECTION
WITH ALL BEINGS.

I AM GUIDED BY MY GOOD FEELINGS.

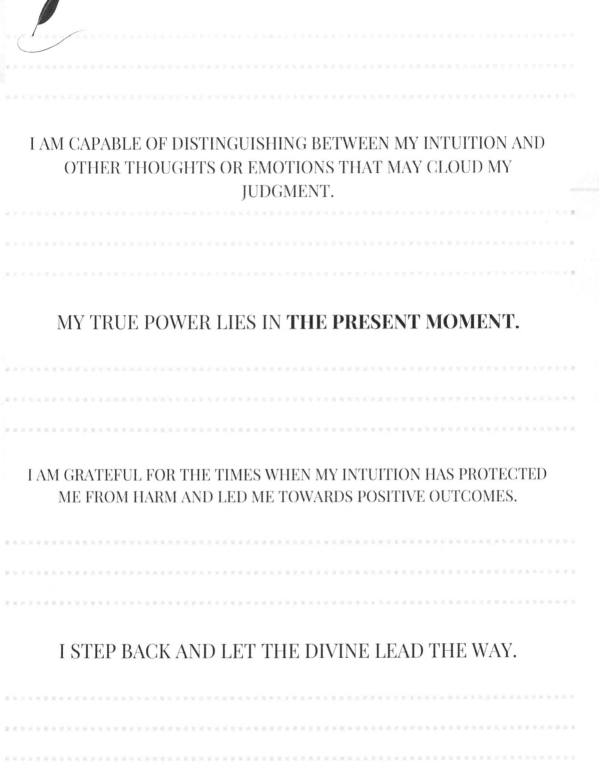

I AM AN ETERNAL AND INFINITE SPIRIT HAVING A
HUMAN EXPERIENCE.

I AM CAPABLE OF DISTINGUISHING BETWEEN MY INTUITION AND
OTHER THOUGHTS OR EMOTIONS THAT MAY CLOUD MY
JUDGMENT.

MY TRUE POWER LIES IN **THE PRESENT MOMENT.**

I AM GRATEFUL FOR THE TIMES WHEN MY INTUITION HAS PROTECTED
ME FROM HARM AND LED ME TOWARDS POSITIVE OUTCOMES.

I STEP BACK AND LET THE DIVINE LEAD THE WAY.

MY INNER VOICE IS A RELIABLE SOURCE OF GUIDANCE
AND DIRECTION.

I TRUST THAT MY INTUITION CAN HELP ME TO RECOGNIZE AND
NAVIGATE THROUGH COMPLEX SITUATIONS AND RELATIONSHIPS.

I AM WILLING TO LEARN THROUGH **LOVE**.

I AM RESPONSIBLE FOR MY SPIRITUAL DEVELOPMENT.

MY BODY IS A LOVELY HOME FOR MY RADIANT SOUL.

190

"The intuitive mind is a sacred gift and the rational mind is a faithful servant. We have created a society that honors the servant and has forgotten the gift."
– Albert Einstein

"INTUITION IS A STRONG FEMININE QUALITY. IT'S LIKE HAVING A SIXTH SENSE."
– GINA LOLLOBRIGIDA

"Intuition is a natural ability that we all have, but it requires attention and cultivation in order to become a reliable tool for decision-making." – Deepak Chopra

"Intuition is a skill that improves with practice."
– Caroline Myss

"Intuition is a spiritual faculty and does not explain, but simply points the way."
– Florence Scovel Shinn

"Intuition is the whisper of the soul."

- Jiddu Krishnamurti

"Intuition is a vital force that allows us to navigate the unknown and create new realities."
– Shakti Gawain

"You will never follow your own inner voice until you clear up the doubts in your mind."
— Roy T. Bennett

"When you reach the end of what you should know, you will be at the beginning of what you should sense."
— Kahlil Gibrán

"I BELIEVE IN INTUITIONS AND INSPIRATIONS...I SOMETIMES FEEL THAT I AM RIGHT. I DO NOT KNOW THAT I AM."
— ALBERT EINSTEIN

"Don't try to comprehend with your mind. Your minds are very limited. Use your intuition." —— Madeleine L'Engle

"Intuition is the highest form of intelligence, transcending all individual abilities and skills." - Sylvia Clare

"INTUITION IS THE VOICE OF THE SPIRIT WITHIN YOU." - WAYNE DYER

Take a deep breath and listen to your inner wisdom and intuition, trusting your hunches and instincts. Every step you take toward your goals is a step in the right direction. Write your affirmations with positivity and hope, knowing that you are on the right track.

Love

LOVE FLOWS FREELY AND ABUNDANTLY **INTO MY LIFE.**

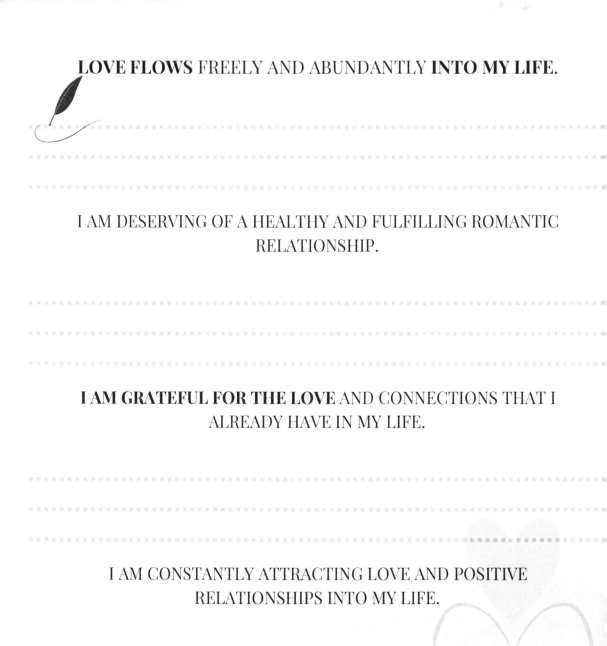

I AM DESERVING OF A HEALTHY AND FULFILLING ROMANTIC RELATIONSHIP.

I AM GRATEFUL FOR THE LOVE AND CONNECTIONS THAT I ALREADY HAVE IN MY LIFE.

I AM CONSTANTLY ATTRACTING LOVE AND POSITIVE RELATIONSHIPS INTO MY LIFE.

I AM HAPPY AND FULFILLED IN MY RELATIONSHIP.

MY HEART IS OPEN.

I AM ATTRACTIVE AND CONFIDENT IN MYSELF AND MY
ABILITY TO ATTRACT LOVE INTO MY LIFE.

I AM DESERVING OF A PARTNER WHO LOVES AND
RESPECTS ME FOR WHO I AM.

I LET GO OF RELATIONSHIPS THAT NO LONGER SERVE ME
AND **MAKE SPACE FOR NEW ONES.**

I AM WORTHY OF EXPERIENCING A DEEP AND MEANINGFUL
CONNECTION WITH MY PARTNER.

I AM OPEN TO NEW EXPERIENCES AND OPPORTUNITIES
TO MEET NEW PEOPLE.

I CHOOSE TO **LOVE MYSELF AND MY PARTNER
WILL LOVE ME TOO.**

I AM GRATEFUL FOR ALL THE LOVE AND AFFECTION I GET.

REAL LOVE STARTS WITH ME.

I AM PATIENT AND UNDERSTANDING IN MY RELATIONSHIPS.

I AM WORTHY OF LOVE AND AFFECTION.

I AM OPEN TO GIVING AND RECEIVING LOVE IN
ALL ITS FORMS.

I RADIATE LOVE AND POSITIVITY TO THOSE AROUND ME.

I TRUST IN THE UNIVERSE TO BRING ME THE **RIGHT
PERSON AT THE RIGHT TIME.**

THE MORE LOVE I GIVE, THE MORE I RECEIVE.

I AM OPEN TO NEW EXPERIENCES THAT BRING ME JOY AND
FULFILLMENT.

I AM GRATEFUL FOR THE LOVE THAT I GIVE AND
RECEIVE IN MY LIFE.

MY RELATIONSHIPS ARE BUILT ON TRUST, HONESTY,
AND AUTHENTICITY.

I AM CONSTANTLY EXPANDING MY CAPACITY TO
LOVE AND BE LOVED.

I AM GRATEFUL FOR THE LOVE AND SUPPORT OF MY
FAMILY AND FRIENDS.

I AM ATTRACTING THE RIGHT PARTNER WHO ALIGNS WITH
MY VALUES AND GOALS.

I AM A QUEEN AT MANIFESTING LOVE AND CREATING POSITIVE
RELATIONSHIPS IN MY LIFE.

I VALUE AND RESPECT THE OPINIONS AND
FEELINGS OF MY PARTNER.

I AM EXCITED AND **OPTIMISTIC** ABOUT THE FUTURE
OF MY RELATIONSHIPS.

MY VIBRATION IS TUNED TO **THE FREQUENCY OF LOVE.**

I AM GRATEFUL FOR THE LOVE THAT I HAVE IN MY LIFE,
WHETHER IT IS FROM FRIENDS, FAMILY, OR MY PARTNER.

I AM WORTHY OF BEING **LOVED** FOR WHO I AM.

MY PARTNER AND I **COMMUNICATE
EFFECTIVELY** AND RESPECTFULLY.

I DESERVE REAL AND AUTHENTIC LOVE.

I LOVE MYSELF FULLY, AND THIS OPENS THE DOOR TO
RECEIVING LOVE FROM OTHERS.

I AM WILLING TO PUT IN THE WORK TO BUILD AND MAINTAIN
HEALTHY AND FULFILLING RELATIONSHIPS.

I ATTRACT PEOPLE INTO MY LIFE WHO BRING ME
JOY AND HAPPINESS.

EVERY SINGLE PART OF ME IS WORTHY OF
UNCONDITIONAL LOVE.

I TRUST IN THE TIMING OF THE UNIVERSE TO BRING
ME THE LOVE I NEED AT THE RIGHT TIME.

I EXPRESS MY EMOTIONS AND FEELINGS IN A
HEALTHY AND CONSTRUCTIVE WAY.

I SHOW AFFECTION AND APPRECIATION TO MY LOVED ONES
REGULARLY.

I RELEASE MY PAST AND AM READY TO FIND LOVE.

I AM WILLING TO COMPROMISE AND WORK ON MY
RELATIONSHIPS.

I CHOOSE **PARTNERS WHO RESPECT AND SUPPORT ME.**

IT IS SAFE FOR ME TO OPEN MY HEART TO ANOTHER.

I MAKE TIME FOR THOSE I LOVE.

I FEEL FREE TO REVEAL **MY TRUE SELF** TO MY PARTNER.

THE LOVE BETWEEN ME AND MY PARTNER IS STRONGER
THAN OUR DISAGREEMENTS.

I AM WILLING TO **TAKE RISKS** AND BE VULNERABLE IN
MY RELATIONSHIPS.

I CHOOSE TO LET GO OF FEAR AND INSECURITIES THAT MAY HOLD ME BACK FROM EXPERIENCING LOVE FULLY.

I AM ABLE TO COMMUNICATE MY NEEDS AND BOUNDARIES IN A HEALTHY WAY.

THERE IS SO MUCH LOVE IN MY LIFE.

I AM WORTHY OF A LOVE THAT IS HONEST, RESPECTFUL, AND FULFILLING, AND I AM WILLING TO WAIT FOR THAT KIND OF LOVE.

I BELIEVE IN **THE POWER OF LOVE** AND ITS ABILITY TO **TRANSFORM MY LIFE.**

I AM WORTHY OF A LOVE THAT IS **PURE AND TRUE.**

I AM ATTRACTING A PARTNER WHO SHARES MY VALUES, INTERESTS, AND GOALS IN LIFE.

I RELEASE ALL NEGATIVE THOUGHTS AND BELIEFS ABOUT LOVE AND EMBRACE A **POSITIVE AND LOVING MINDSET.**

I AM LOVE, AND I RADIATE LOVE IN ALL AREAS OF MY LIFE.

I AM WHOLE AND COMPLETE ON MY OWN, AND I SHARE MY LOVE WITH SOMEONE WHO COMPLEMENTS AND ENHANCES MY LIFE.

"Being deeply loved by someone gives you strength, while loving someone deeply gives you courage." - Lao Tzu

"IT IS BETTER TO BE HATED FOR WHAT YOU ARE THAN TO BE LOVED FOR WHAT YOU ARE NOT." — ANDRE GIDE

"There is never a time or place for true love. It happens accidentally, in a heartbeat, in a single flashing, throbbing moment." — Sarah Dessen

"Love is not about possession, it's about appreciation." - Unknown

"WHERE THERE IS LOVE THERE IS LIFE." MAHATMA GANDHI

"LOVE IS THE FLOWER YOU'VE GOT TO LET GROW." - JOHN LENNON

"You've gotta dance like there's nobody watching,
Love like you'll never be hurt,
Sing like there's nobody listening,
And live like it's heaven on earth." — William W. Purkey

"Love is that condition in which the happiness of another person is essential to your own." — Robert A. Heinlein

"Let the beauty of what you love be what you do." — Rumi

"Love is not about how much you say 'I love you', but how much you can prove that it's true." – Unknown

"In the end, only three things matter: how much you loved, how gently you lived, and how gracefully you let go of things not meant for you." –Buddha

"I LOVE YOU NOT ONLY FOR WHAT YOU ARE, BUT FOR WHAT I AM WHEN I AM WITH YOU. I LOVE YOU NOT ONLY FOR WHAT YOU HAVE MADE OF YOURSELF, BUT FOR WHAT YOU ARE MAKING OF ME. I LOVE YOU FOR THE PART OF ME THAT YOU BRING OUT." — ELIZABETH BARRETT BROWNING

Take a deep breath, close your eyes, and think about the love you want to attract into your life. Now, write down your affirmations with passion and sincerity, knowing that the universe is listening and ready to bring you the love you deserve.

Overcoming Anxiety

I AM CALM AND CENTERED, EVEN IN THE FACE OF UNCERTAINTY.

I AM CAPABLE OF HANDLING ANY SITUATION THAT COMES MY WAY.

I KNOW **IT'S OKAY** TO GET OUT OF MY COMFORT ZONE.

I AM CAPABLE OF SLOWING DOWN AND TAKING **DEEP BREATHS TO CALM MY MIND AND BODY.**

AS I RELAX AND SLOW MY BREATHING, ANXIETY
FLOWS OUT.

I LET GO OF THE THINGS THAT TRIGGER MY ANXIETY AND FOCUS
ON THE THINGS THAT BRING ME JOY AND PEACE.

I INHALE PEACE AND EXHALE WORRY.

I AM CAPABLE OF FACING MY FEARS AND
OVERCOMING THEM, ONE STEP AT A TIME.

I FIND JOY AND HAPPINESS IN THE PRESENT MOMENT.

I HAVE POWER OVER MY MIND, NOT EXTERNAL EVENTS.

I AM CAPABLE OF FINDING PEACE AND CALM WITHIN MYSELF,
EVEN WHEN EXTERNAL CIRCUMSTANCES ARE CHALLENGING.

I AM EMPOWERED TO CHALLENGE THE NEGATIVE
THOUGHTS AND BELIEFS.

**I AM IN CONTROL OF MY THOUGHTS AND
EMOTIONS,** AND I CHOOSE PEACE.

MY STATE OF MIND DEPENDS ON ME AND I CAN CHANGE IT
WHENEVER I WANT.

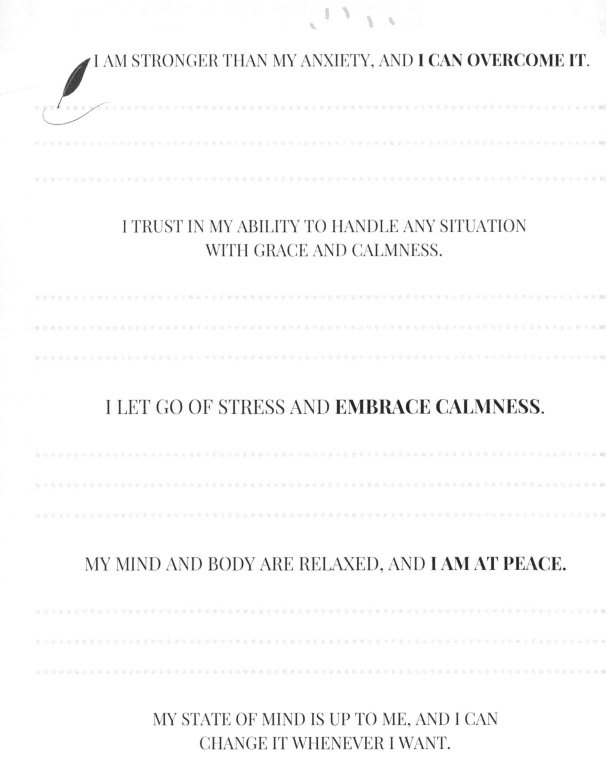

I AM STRONGER THAN MY ANXIETY, AND **I CAN OVERCOME IT.**

I TRUST IN MY ABILITY TO HANDLE ANY SITUATION
WITH GRACE AND CALMNESS.

I LET GO OF STRESS AND **EMBRACE CALMNESS**.

MY MIND AND BODY ARE RELAXED, AND **I AM AT PEACE.**

MY STATE OF MIND IS UP TO ME, AND I CAN
CHANGE IT WHENEVER I WANT.

CIRCUMSTANCES DO NOT PROVOKE MY ANXIETY.

I AM SURROUNDED BY POSITIVE ENERGY AND LIGHT,
WHICH HELP ME TO OVERCOME ANXIETY.

I AM IN TUNE WITH MY **INNER PEACE** AND TRUST IN IT.

I CAN QUIET MY MIND IN EVERY SITUATION.

I AM WORTHY OF SELF-CARE AND TAKING TIME FOR MYSELF
TO MANAGE MY ANXIETY AND STRESS.

I AM CENTERED AND GROUNDED, EVEN IN THE MIDST OF CHAOS.

ALL IS WELL WITH MY SOUL.

I BREATHE DEEPLY AND FEEL **CALMNESS WASH OVER ME**.

I CHOOSE TO LIVE IN THE PRESENT MOMENT AND LET GO
OF WORRIES ABOUT THE FUTURE.

INSIDE ME LIES A GREAT RESERVOIR OF CALMNESS.

WHEN I'M FEELING OVERWHELMED, I ALLOW MYSELF SPACE TO
PAUSE AND BREATHE.

I AM SAFE AND PROTECTED, AND EVERYTHING WILL
WORK OUT FOR MY HIGHEST GOOD.

I ALWAYS STAY POSITIVE IN INTIMIDATING SOCIAL SITUATIONS.

I AM CONFIDENT IN MY ABILITY TO FACE MY FEARS AND
OVERCOME THEM WITH COURAGE AND DETERMINATION.

MY BREATH IS MY BEST GUIDE WHEN I NEED TO
FIND BALANCE AND PEACE OF MIND.

I LET GO OF NEGATIVE THOUGHTS AND FOCUS ON POSITIVITY.

I AM GRATEFUL FOR THE QUIET MOMENTS OF PEACE
AND SOLITUDE IN MY LIFE.

I AM CAPABLE OF OVERCOMING MY ANXIETY AND LIVING
A FULFILLING LIFE.

I AM AT PEACE WITH MYSELF, MY PAST, AND MY FUTURE.

I MAKE MINDFULNESS AND MEDITATION PRACTICES
PART OF MY DAILY ROUTINE TO REDUCE ANXIETY.

I AM AT PEACE WITH WHO I AM AND WHERE I AM IN LIFE.

I HOLD SPACE FOR MYSELF AND **HONOR MY NEEDS.**

I AM IN CONTROL OF MY REACTIONS AND CHOOSE TO
RESPOND CALMLY IN ANY SITUATION.

MY MIND AND BODY ARE RELAXED, AND I AM
FREE FROM STRESS.

MY HEART IS GRATEFUL AND MY MIND IS AT PEACE.

DEEP INNER PEACE IS MY NATURAL STATE.

MY INNER PEACE IS A REFLECTION OF **MY STRENGTH AND RESILIENCE.**

I AM CENTERED, GROUNDED, AND AT PEACE WITHIN MYSELF.

I AM WORTHY OF SEEKING HELP AND SUPPORT FROM OTHERS WHEN I NEED IT.

MY INNER PEACE **IS UNSHAKEABLE,** AND I AM AT EASE NO MATTER WHAT.

I RELEASE ALL TENSION AND WELCOME INNER PEACE.

EVEN WHEN THE WORLD AROUND ME FEELS CHAOTIC,
I REMAIN ROOTED FIRMLY TO THE GROUND.

I CHOOSE TO CULTIVATE GRATITUDE AND FOCUS ON THE
POSITIVE ASPECTS OF MY LIFE.

THERE IS BEAUTY TO BE FOUND IN SLOWING DOWN.

I RELEASE THE NEED TO CONTROL MY LIFE AND SURRENDER
TO THIS PRESENT MOMENT.

I ACCEPT THINGS AS THEY ARE, AND I FIND PEACE IN
THAT ACCEPTANCE.

I AM FREE FROM ANXIETY AND STRESS.

I AM GRATEFUL FOR THE PEOPLE AND THINGS THAT
BRING ME PEACE.

I AM WORTHY OF PRACTICING SELF–ACCEPTANCE AND
EMBRACING MY IMPERFECTIONS AND FLAWS.

I BREATH PEACE, I FEEL PEACE, AND I LIVE IN PEACE.

"FEELINGS COME AND GO LIKE CLOUDS IN A WINDY SKY. CONSCIOUS BREATHING IS MY ANCHOR."
—THICH NHAT HANH

"Let your mind and heart rest for a while. You will catch up, the world will not stop spinning for you, but you will catch up. Take a rest."
— Cynthia Go

"NOTHING IN THE AFFAIRS OF MEN IS WORTHY OF GREAT ANXIETY."
—PLATO

"How much pain have cost us the evils which have never happened." —Thomas Jefferson

"YOU ARE BIGGER THAN WHAT IT MAKING YOU ANXIOUS."
– UNKNOWN

"You don't have to control your thoughts; you just have to stop letting them control you."
—Dan Millman

"If you feel like you're losing everything, remember trees lose their leaves every year and they stand tall and wait for better days to come." - Unknown

Breathe darling. This is just a chapter. It's not your whole story."
– S.C. Lourie

"DO WHAT YOU CAN, WITH WHAT YOU'VE GOT, WHERE YOU ARE."
—THEODORE ROOSEVELT

"Stress is an ignorant state. It believes that everything is an emergency. Nothing is that important." —Natalie Goldberg

"There is only one way to happiness and that is to cease worrying about things which are beyond the power of our will." – Epictetus

"Your mountain may be harder to climb, but oh the view is divine." – Jennae Cecelia

"Anxiety does not empty tomorrow of its sorrows, but only empties today of its strength."
—Charles Spurgeon

Begin by taking a deep breath, inhaling positivity and exhaling negativity. As you focus on your breath, visualize a sense of calm washing over you, releasing any tension or anxiety you may be feeling. Now, write down your affirmations with conviction and belief, reminding yourself that you have the strength and resilience to overcome anxiety.

Good Friendships

I AM GRATEFUL FOR THE SUPPORTIVE AND
LOVING FRIENDS IN MY LIFE.

I ATTRACT **POSITIVE AND UPLIFTING PEOPLE** INTO MY
LIFE.

MY FRIENDSHIPS ARE BUILT ON TRUST, RESPECT,
AND MUTUAL UNDERSTANDING.

I AM SURROUNDED BY FRIENDS WHO ENCOURAGE AND SUPPORT
ME THROUGH BOTH GOOD TIMES AND BAD.

MY FRIENDSHIPS ARE HEALTHY AND BALANCED,
WITH **BOTH GIVE AND TAKE.**

I APPRECIATE AND CELEBRATE THE DIFFERENCES BETWEEN
MYSELF AND MY FRIENDS.

I FORGIVE MY FRIENDS FOR THEIR MISTAKES AND
THEY FORGIVE ME FOR MINE.

I ALLOW MY FRIENDS TO **BE PERFECT WITH**
THEIR **IMPERFECTIONS.**

I'M LIKE A MAGNET WHEN IT COMES TO MAKING FRIENDS.

I AM ALWAYS LEARNING AND GROWING THROUGH
MY FRIENDSHIPS.

I TRUST THAT **MY FRIENDS HAVE MY BEST
INTERESTS AT HEART.**

I AM ABLE TO BE MYSELF AROUND MY FRIENDS AND FEEL
ACCEPTED AND LOVED.

I AM SURROUNDED BY FRIENDS WHO ARE POSITIVE,
UPLIFTING, AND INSPIRING.

I LOVE OTHERS AROUND ME AS THEY ARE.

MY FRIENDS BRING OUT THE BEST IN ME, AND I
BRING OUT THE BEST IN THEM.

I AM DESERVING OF FRIENDS WHO APPRECIATE AND
VALUE ME FOR WHO I AM.

I COMMUNICATE OPENLY AND HONESTLY WITH MY
FRIENDS, AND THEY DO THE SAME WITH ME.

MY FRIENDS INSPIRE ME TO BE MY BEST SELF AND
PURSUE MY DREAMS.

I PUT MY TRUST IN NATURE FOR PROVIDING ME WITH
THE RIGHT FRIENDS AT THE DESIRED TIMES.

I AM A LOYAL AND DEPENDABLE FRIEND TO THOSE I
CARE ABOUT.

I TRUST MY FRIENDS WITH MY HEART.

BEING LOVEABLE AROUND OTHERS REQUIRES **LOVING
MYSELF FIRST!**

MY FRIENDS ARE WORTH ALL THE EFFORTS AND
SINCERITY.

I AM GRATEFUL FOR THE MEMORIES AND EXPERIENCES I HAVE
SHARED WITH MY FRIENDS.

I AM RESPECTED AND LOVED BY MY FRIENDS.

I AM THANKFUL FOR ALL OF MY WONDERFUL FRIENDS.

I SHOW UP FOR MY FRIENDS AND SUPPORT THEM IN
THEIR GOALS AND DREAMS.

I AM A GOOD LISTENER AND ABLE TO PROVIDE SUPPORT TO MY
FRIENDS WHEN THEY NEED IT.

MY FRIENDSHIPS ARE A SOURCE OF **STRENGTH AND
HAPPINESS** IN MY LIFE.

MAKING NEW FRIENDSHIPS IS VERY EASY FOR ME.

PEOPLE FEEL COMFORTABLE INTERACTING WITH ME.

I ATTRACT LASTING FRIENDSHIPS.

I HAVE HEALTHY BOUNDARIES IN MY ENTIRE FRIEND CIRCLE.

I RESORT TO MAKING PEACE WITH MY FRIEND
DESPITE ANY CONFLICTS.

I'M SURROUNDED BY THE LOVE OF MY FRIENDS.

I DON'T JUDGE MY FRIENDS.

PEOPLE I COME ACROSS EVERY DAY **ARE WARM AND FRIENDLY TO ME.**

WITH EACH PASSING DAY, MY CIRCLE OF FRIENDS EXPANDS.

I ATTRACT A DIVERSE AND SUPPORTIVE NETWORK OF FRIENDS WHO ENRICH MY LIFE IN DIFFERENT WAYS.

I CHOOSE TO LET GO OF JEALOUSY AND COMPARISON
IN MY FRIENDSHIPS.

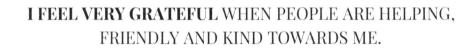

I FEEL VERY GRATEFUL WHEN PEOPLE ARE HELPING,
FRIENDLY AND KIND TOWARDS ME.

A SIMPLE SMILE FROM OTHER FRIENDS
MAKES MY DAY BETTER.

WITTY, GENUINE AND GOOD PEOPLE KEEP COMING INTO MY LIFE.

I'M GRATEFUL FOR THE COMPANY OF MY CLOSE FRIENDS.

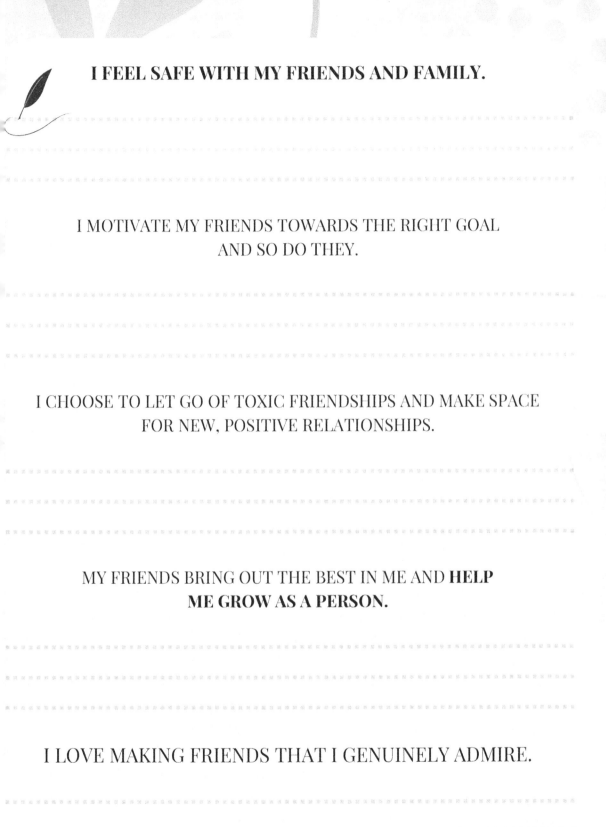

I FEEL SAFE WITH MY FRIENDS AND FAMILY.

I MOTIVATE MY FRIENDS TOWARDS THE RIGHT GOAL
AND SO DO THEY.

I CHOOSE TO LET GO OF TOXIC FRIENDSHIPS AND MAKE SPACE
FOR NEW, POSITIVE RELATIONSHIPS.

MY FRIENDS BRING OUT THE BEST IN ME AND **HELP
ME GROW AS A PERSON.**

I LOVE MAKING FRIENDS THAT I GENUINELY ADMIRE.

EVERY DAY, POSITIVE AND AMAZING PEOPLE ENTER MY
LIFE AND LEAVE THEIR MARKS.

NEW PEOPLE DON'T MAKE ME UNCOMFORTABLE.

I PICK ONLY THE BEST PEOPLE TO MAKE FRIENDS WITH.

MY FRIENDS AND FAMILY CELEBRATE MY UNIQUENESS AND
ENCOURAGE ME TO BE MY AUTHENTIC SELF.

ALL THE PEOPLE I ATTRACT ARE FUN AND UPBEAT.

ANY TOXIC PEOPLE IN MY LIFE I LEAVE BEHIND.

THE CONNECTIONS I SHARE WITH THOSE I KNOW **ARE DEEP.**

MY FRIENDS ARE MY COMFORT IN DARK TIMES.

I LET MY FRIENDS KNOW THAT THEY MATTER TO ME.

I ALWAYS MAKE THE RIGHT FRIENDS AT THE RIGHT TIME.

Friendship is another word for love. -Unknown

"True friendship comes when the silence between two people is comfortable." - David Tyson

"A true friend is someone who knows the song in your heart and can sing it back to you when you have forgotten the words." - Donna Roberts

"FRIENDS ARE THE FAMILY WE CHOOSE FOR OURSELVES." - EDNA BUCHANAN

A friend is someone who makes it easy to believe in yourself. -Heidi Wills

"A FRIEND IS ONE OF THE NICEST THINGS YOU CAN HAVE, AND ONE OF THE BEST THINGS YOU CAN BE." - WINNIE THE POOH

"FRIENDSHIP IS A SHELTERING TREE." - SAMUEL TAYLOR COLERIDGE

"Friendship is born at that moment when one person says to another: 'What! You too? I thought I was the only one.'" - C.S. Lewis

"A friend is someone who understands your past, believes in your future, and accepts you just the way you are." - Unknown

Keep the ones that heard you when you never said a word. -Unknown

"There are no strangers here; Only friends you haven't yet met." - William Butler Yeats

"The language of friendship is not words but meanings." - Henry David Thoreau

A friend is someone who gives you total freedom to be yourself -Jim Morrison

"Many people will walk in and out of your life, but only true friends will leave footprints in your heart." - Eleanor Roosevelt

"A true friend is someone who reaches for your hand and touches your heart." - Heather Pryor

Take a moment to think about the kind of friendships you want to attract into your life. Visualize yourself surrounded by positive, supportive and uplifting people who share your values and aspirations. With each affirmation, feel gratitude for the friendships you already have and those to come.

Creativity

MY CREATIVE ENERGY IS BOUNDLESS AND UNLIMITED.

I AM A NATURAL BORN CREATOR AND MY CREATIVE
IDEAS ARE CONSTANTLY FLOWING.

I AM OPEN TO EXPLORING NEW CREATIVE MEDIUMS AND
TECHNIQUES.

I FIND INSPIRATION AND CREATIVITY IN EVERY
ASPECT OF MY LIFE.

I AM CONSTANTLY DISCOVERING **NEW IDEAS**
AND WAYS OF THINKING.

MY CREATIVE PROJECTS ARE **EXPRESSIONS OF MY**
INNERMOST **THOUGHTS AND EMOTIONS**.

INNOVATIVE IDEAS FIND THEIR WAY INTO MY LIFE.

MY CREATIVITY IS AN IMPORTANT PART OF WHO I AM
AND I HONOR IT.

I AM CAPABLE OF TURNING MY CREATIVE IDEAS INTO REALITY.

MY CREATIVITY HAS THE POWER TO INSPIRE AND
BRING JOY TO OTHERS.

I AM CONSTANTLY **EXPANDING MY CREATIVE
HORIZONS** AND TRYING NEW THINGS.

I AM PROUD OF MY UNIQUE AND CREATIVE
PERSPECTIVE ON LIFE.

I AM OPEN TO RECEIVING CONSTRUCTIVE FEEDBACK AND
USING IT TO IMPROVE MY CREATIVITY.

MY IMAGINATION KNOWS NO BOUNDS, AND I CAN
VISUALIZE ANYTHING I DESIRE.

I WELCOME AND EMBRACE CREATIVE CHALLENGES
AND OPPORTUNITIES.

MY CREATIVE VISION IS POWERFUL AND CAPABLE
OF MAKING A POSITIVE IMPACT.

MY CREATIVITY IS FUELED BY PASSION, CURIOSITY,
AND JOY.

MY CREATIVITY IS AN INTEGRAL PART OF MY LIFE
AND MY IDENTITY.

MY CREATIVITY **IS LIMITLESS,** AND THERE IS
ALWAYS MORE TO EXPLORE.

I GIVE MYSELF PERMISSION TO CREATE WITHOUT SELF-DOUBT OR JUDGMENT.

MY CREATIVITY **IS NOT LIMITED BY TIME OR SPACE.**

MY CREATIVE ENDEAVORS ARE ALIGNED WITH MY PURPOSE AND VALUES.

I TRUST THAT MY CREATIVE IDEAS WILL MANIFEST INTO SOMETHING AMAZING.

I ALLOW MY INTUITION TO GUIDE ME TOWARDS MY MOST CREATIVE IDEAS.

I AM FEARLESS IN EXPLORING NEW CREATIVE PATHS AND
PUSHING BOUNDARIES.

MY CREATIVITY SPARKS **JOY AND EXCITEMENT** IN MY LIFE.

I AM CONNECTED TO THE CREATIVE UNIVERSE AND
RECEIVE INSPIRATION EVERY DAY.

I CAN ENTER INTO A CREATIVE STATE OF MIND
WHENEVER I WANT TO.

I AM ALWAYS LEARNING AND GROWING IN MY
CREATIVE JOURNEY.

EVERY DAY, I FEEL AMAZING BECAUSE **I PRODUCE.**

I AM AN ARTIST IN MY OWN UNIQUE WAY AND
MY CREATIVITY IS VALUABLE.

I TRUST MY CREATIVE INSTINCTS AND FOLLOW
THEM FEARLESSLY.

MY IDEAS ARE REFRESHING AND NEW.

MY IMAGINATION IS LIMITLESS AND MY CREATIVITY
KNOWS NO BOUNDS.

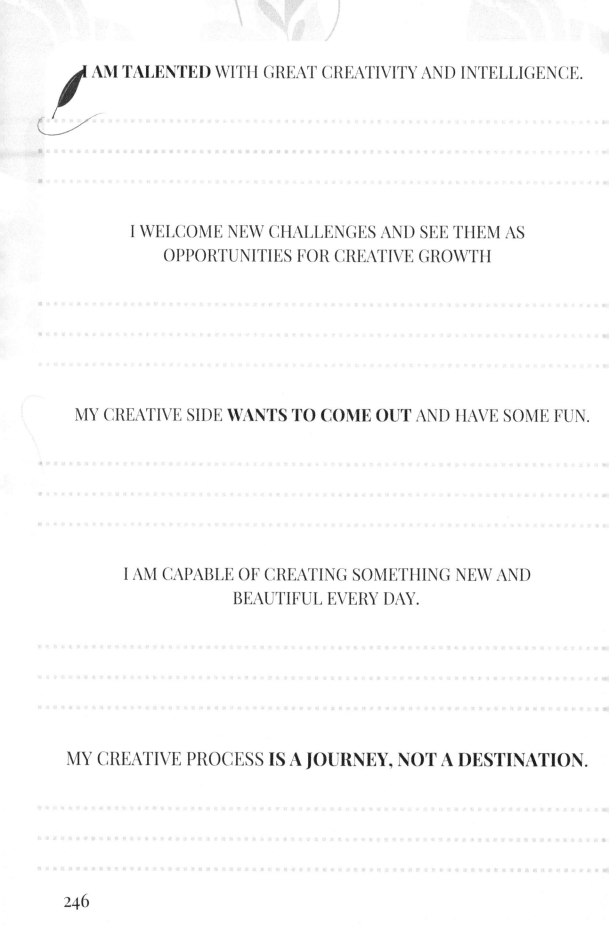

I AM TALENTED WITH GREAT CREATIVITY AND INTELLIGENCE.

I WELCOME NEW CHALLENGES AND SEE THEM AS
OPPORTUNITIES FOR CREATIVE GROWTH

MY CREATIVE SIDE **WANTS TO COME OUT** AND HAVE SOME FUN.

I AM CAPABLE OF CREATING SOMETHING NEW AND
BEAUTIFUL EVERY DAY.

MY CREATIVE PROCESS **IS A JOURNEY, NOT A DESTINATION.**

246

I CAN'T WAIT TO WAKE UP EVERY DAY AND START CREATING

I EMBRACE THE UNKNOWN AND TRUST THAT MY
CREATIVITY WILL GUIDE ME.

I ALLOW MY IMAGINATION TO RUN WILD AND CREATE
AMAZING THINGS.

I AM GRATEFUL FOR THE UNIQUE TALENTS AND ABILITIES
THAT FUEL MY CREATIVITY.

MY CREATIVE PROJECTS ARE A SOURCE OF PRIDE AND
FULFILLMENT.

I AM AN UNLIMITED CREATIVE CREATURE.

BEING CREATIVE MAKES ME SO ALIVE.

I AM FEARLESS IN EXPLORING NEW IDEAS AND
TAKING CREATIVE RISKS.

I AM SURROUNDED BY BEAUTY AND **FIND
INSPIRATION IN THE WORLD AROUND ME.**

EVERY DAY, CREATIVE ENERGY RUNS THROUGH ME.

MY BRAIN IS PREDISPOSED TO BE CREATIVE.

EVERYTHING AROUND ME INSPIRES ME.

I AM A PIONEER.

I TRUST THAT MY CREATIVE IDEAS WILL LEAD ME TO
SUCCESS AND HAPPINESS.

**I LOVE THE FREEDOM THAT CREATIVE
THINKING GIVES ME.**

I AM FILLED WITH INSPIRATION AND NEW IDEAS EVERY DAY.

MY CREATIVITY INSPIRES ME TO BE MY BEST SELF.

I HONOR MY UNIQUE CREATIVE VOICE AND ALLOW
IT TO BE HEARD.

I AM A CHANNEL FOR DIVINE INSPIRATION AND CREATIVITY.

MY MIND IS FREE TO GO WILD.

"CREATIVITY IS INTELLIGENCE HAVING FUN." - ALBERT EINSTEIN

"You use a glass mirror to see your face. You use works of art to see your soul."
— George Bernard Shaw

"The desire to create is one of the deepest yearnings of the human soul."
— Dieter F. Uchtdorf

"TO BE CREATIVE MEANS TO BE IN LOVE WITH LIFE." - OSHO

CREATIVITY IS JUST CONNECTING THINGS.
- STEVE JOBS

"The chief enemy of creativity is 'good' sense." - Pablo Picasso

"Creativity is inventing, experimenting, growing, taking risks, breaking rules, making mistakes, and having fun."
— Mary Lou Cook

"A creative life is an amplified life. It's a bigger life, a happier life, an expanded life, and a hell of a lot more interesting life"
— Elizabeth Gilbert

"CREATIVITY IS SEEING WHAT OTHERS SEE AND THINKING WHAT NO ONE ELSE EVER THOUGHT."
- ALBERT EINSTEIN

"The worst enemy to creativity is self-doubt."
- Sylvia Plath

"The creative process is a process of surrender, not control."
- Bruce Lee

"IT'S NO GOOD BEING TOO EASILY SWAYED BY PEOPLE'S OPINIONS. YOU HAVE TO BELIEVE IN YOURSELF." - DONATELLA VERSACE

"Great things are done by a series of small things brought together."
— Vincent Van Gogh

"Take a deep breath and let your mind wander to the endless possibilities of your imagination. As you write your affirmations, let your creativity flow freely and without judgment, allowing yourself to tap into your deepest wells of inspiration. Believe in your own creative abilities, knowing that you have a unique perspective to offer the world.

Personal Spiritual Growth

I KNOW THAT **I EXIST FOR A DIVINE PURPOSE**.

EVERYTHING I SEEK IS NOW SEEKING ME.

I AM GRATEFUL FOR ALL THE PEOPLE AND EXPERIENCES
THAT HAVE HELPED ME GROW AND EVOLVE.

I AM COMMITTED TO **SELF-IMPROVEMENT** AND BEING
THE BEST VERSION OF MYSELF.

ALL THAT HAPPENS AROUND ME WILL TEACH ME SOMETHING.

I BELIEVE IN MY ABILITY TO OVERCOME CHALLENGES AND GROW FROM THEM.

I AM PATIENT WITH MYSELF AS I WORK TOWARDS MY PERSONAL GROWTH.

MY MINDSET FRAMES MY REALITY.

I PUT MY LIFE IN THE HANDS OF INFINITE LOVE AND DIVINE WISDOM.

I TRUST THAT **I AM ON THE RIGHT PATH** AND THAT
EVERYTHING IS UNFOLDING EXACTLY AS IT SHOULD.

MY INNER PEACE AND CLARITY GUIDE ME
TOWARDS THE RIGHT PATH.

THE ENTIRE CREATION IS CONSPIRING FOR MY BENEFIT.

ALL IS WELL IN MY WORLD, AS IT SHOULD BE.

I ACKNOWLEDGE MY OWN STRENGTHS AND WEAKNESSES,
AND USE THEM TO MY ADVANTAGE.

ALL OF MY THOUGHTS, WORDS, AND ACTIONS **ARE INFLUENCED BY THE DIVINE.**

I KNOW I CAN ACHIEVE A HIGHER STATE OF CONSCIOUSNESS WITH THE UNIVERSE'S HELP.

I HAVE THE STRENGTH AND RESILIENCE TO OVERCOME OBSTACLES AND CHALLENGES.

I AM GRATEFUL FOR MY PAST EXPERIENCES BECAUSE THEY HELPED SHAPE WHO I AM TODAY.

I AM ALWAYS LOOKING FOR WAYS TO IMPROVE MYSELF, WHETHER IT'S THROUGH EDUCATION, COACHING, OR PERSONAL DEVELOPMENT.

POSITIVE ENERGY FLOWS TO ME AND FLOWS FROM ME.

I PAY MORE ATTENTION TO LISTENING THAN TO SPEAKING.

**MY LIFE IS SATURATED WITH THE GRATITUDE
AND COMPASSION OF GOD.**

I AM WILLING TO ACCEPT MIRACLES THAT EXCEED MY
EXPECTATIONS.

I AM COMMITTED TO PRACTICING SELF-CARE AS A WAY TO
SUPPORT MY PERSONAL GROWTH.

I AM ALIGNED WITH MY HIGHER PURPOSE.

I AM CONSTANTLY LEARNING, GROWING, AND EXPANDING MY MIND.

I KNOW WHAT IS RIGHT FOR ME IN MY HEART AND WHO I AM.

I AM CONSTANTLY LEARNING AND GROWING, BOTH PERSONALLY AND PROFESSIONALLY.

I AM IN CONTROL OF MY THOUGHTS AND EMOTIONS, AND I CHOOSE TO FOCUS ON POSITIVITY AND GROWTH.

I EMBRACE CHANGE AS A NATURAL PART OF LIFE
AND USE IT TO MY ADVANTAGE.

I ALLOW REST, SECURITY, AND LOVE TO WASH OVER ME.

I VALUE MY OWN GROWTH.

EVERY DAY, I AM BECOMING A BETTER VERSION OF MYSELF.

MY DOWNFALLS ARE GIFTS THAT STRENGTHEN ME
AND HELP ME BECOME A BETTER AND WISER WOMAN.

I TAKE TIME TO REFLECT ON MY EXPERIENCES
AND LEARN FROM THEM.

I AM WILLING TO TAKE RISKS AND **STEP OUTSIDE OF
MY COMFORT ZONE TO GROW.**

LIFE IS A BEAUTIFUL GIFT.

EVERYTHING IN LIFE HAPPENS FOR A REASON.

I DON'T FOCUS ON THE PROBLEMS BECAUSE
THEY ARE ILLUSIONS.

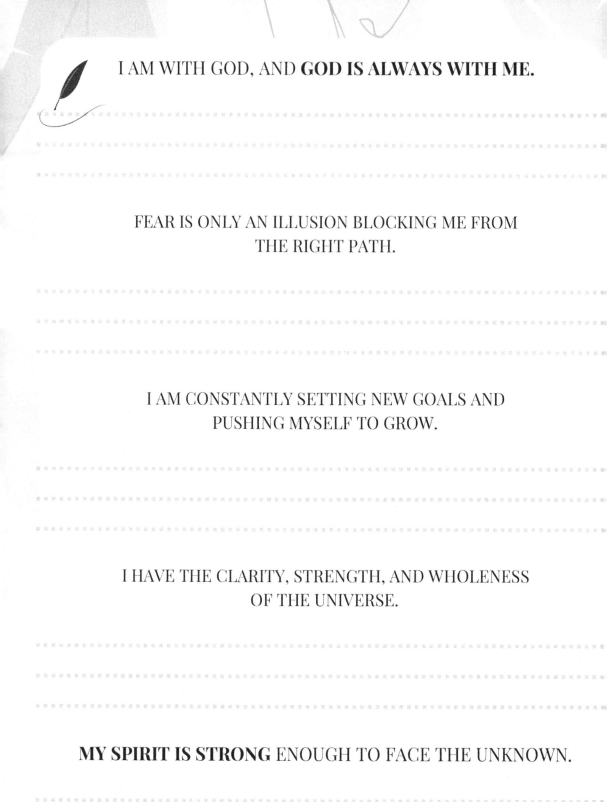

I AM WITH GOD, AND **GOD IS ALWAYS WITH ME.**

FEAR IS ONLY AN ILLUSION BLOCKING ME FROM
THE RIGHT PATH.

I AM CONSTANTLY SETTING NEW GOALS AND
PUSHING MYSELF TO GROW.

I HAVE THE CLARITY, STRENGTH, AND WHOLENESS
OF THE UNIVERSE.

MY SPIRIT IS STRONG ENOUGH TO FACE THE UNKNOWN.

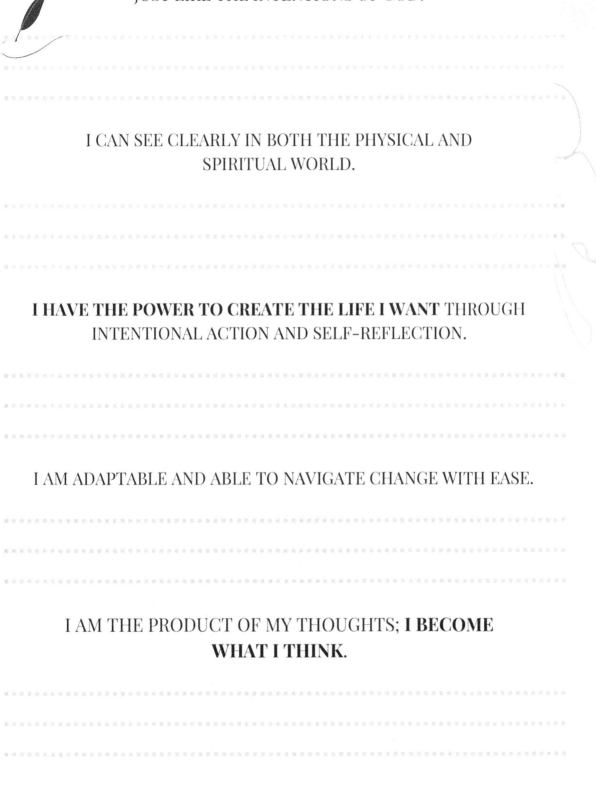

MY THOUGHTS ARE POSITIVE AND LOVING,
JUST LIKE THE INTENTIONS OF GOD.

I CAN SEE CLEARLY IN BOTH THE PHYSICAL AND
SPIRITUAL WORLD.

I HAVE THE POWER TO CREATE THE LIFE I WANT THROUGH
INTENTIONAL ACTION AND SELF-REFLECTION.

I AM ADAPTABLE AND ABLE TO NAVIGATE CHANGE WITH EASE.

I AM THE PRODUCT OF MY THOUGHTS; **I BECOME
WHAT I THINK.**

263

I AM OPEN TO RECEIVING **FEEDBACK** AND USING IT **TO IMPROVE.**

I AM MINDFUL AND INTENTIONAL ABOUT MY PERSONAL GROWTH AND DEVELOPMENT.

I ACKNOWLEDGE GOD IN EVERY CREATION.

GOD MADE ME UNIQUE AND IS ALWAYS BY MY SIDE.

I HAVE A MISSION TO ACCOMPLISH, AND I MUST DO SO.

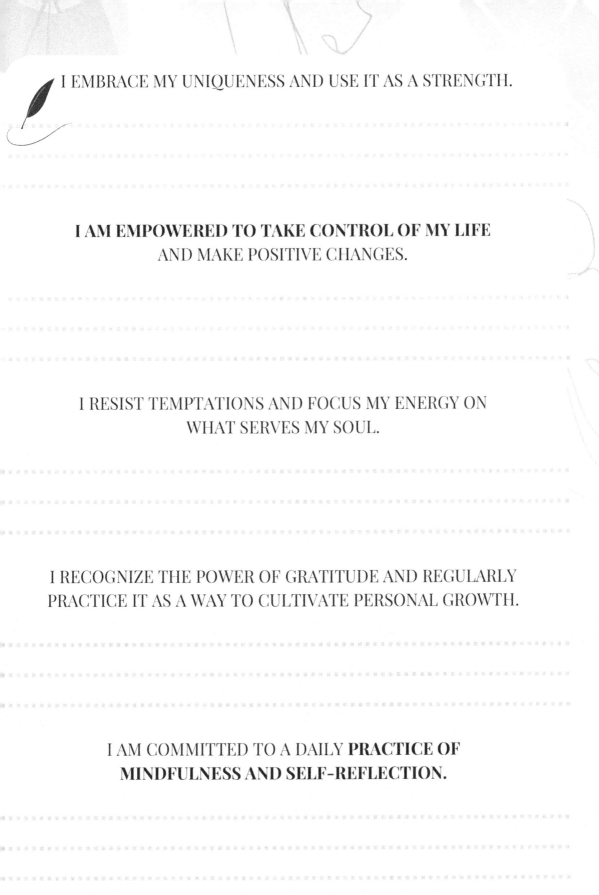

I EMBRACE MY UNIQUENESS AND USE IT AS A STRENGTH.

I AM EMPOWERED TO TAKE CONTROL OF MY LIFE
AND MAKE POSITIVE CHANGES.

I RESIST TEMPTATIONS AND FOCUS MY ENERGY ON
WHAT SERVES MY SOUL.

I RECOGNIZE THE POWER OF GRATITUDE AND REGULARLY
PRACTICE IT AS A WAY TO CULTIVATE PERSONAL GROWTH.

I AM COMMITTED TO A DAILY **PRACTICE OF
MINDFULNESS AND SELF-REFLECTION.**

"By doing the work to love ourselves more, I believe we will love each other better." – Laverne Cox

"DO THE BEST YOU CAN UNTIL YOU KNOW BETTER. THEN WHEN YOU KNOW BETTER, DO BETTER." - MAYA ANGELOU

"Life's challenges are not supposed to paralyze you, they're supposed to help you discover who you are." - Bernice Johnson Reagon

"IF YOU WANT TO CHANGE THE WORLD, CHANGE YOURSELF." – MAHATMA GANDHI

"You are the master of your destiny. You can influence, direct and control your own environment." – Napoleon Hill

"IN ORDER TO BE IRREPLACEABLE, ONE MUST ALWAYS BE DIFFERENT." - COCO CHANEL

"Don't go through life, grow through life." - Eric Butterworth

"YOUR TIME IS LIMITED. DON'T WASTE IT LIVING SOMEONE ELSE'S LIFE." - STEVE JOBS

"the more that you read, the more things you will know. the more that you learn, the more places you'll go." - Dr. Seuss

"Stay afraid, but do it anyway. What's important is the action. You don't have to wait to be confident. Just do it and eventually the confidence will follow." – Carrie Fisher

"Take criticism seriously, but not personally. If there is truth or merit in the criticism, try to learn from it. Otherwise, let it roll right off you." - Hillary Clinton

WE ARE PRODUCTS OF OUR PAST. BUT WE DON'T HAVE TO BE PRISONERS OF IT." – RICK WARREN

"Recognizing that you are not where you want to be is a starting point to begin changing your life." – Deborah Day

"There is nothing noble in being superior to your fellow man; true nobility is being superior to your former self. - Ernest Hemingway

Take a moment to reflect on your personal journey and the areas of your life where you want to grow and improve. As you write your affirmations, focus on cultivating a mindset of growth and self-improvement, knowing that every challenge is an opportunity for learning and development. Trust in your own ability to overcome obstacles and embrace change, and believe in your capacity to become the best version of yourself.

Self-Care and Self-Love

TAKING CARE OF MYSELF IS NOT SELFISH, IT IS NECESSARY.

I RESPECT MY OWN NEEDS AND PRIORITIES BY SAYING
NO WHEN IT IS RIGHT FOR ME.

I LOVE MYSELF. I BELIEVE IN MYSELF. I SUPPORT MYSELF.

I HONOR MY EMOTIONS AND ALLOW MYSELF TO FEEL
AND PROCESS THEM.

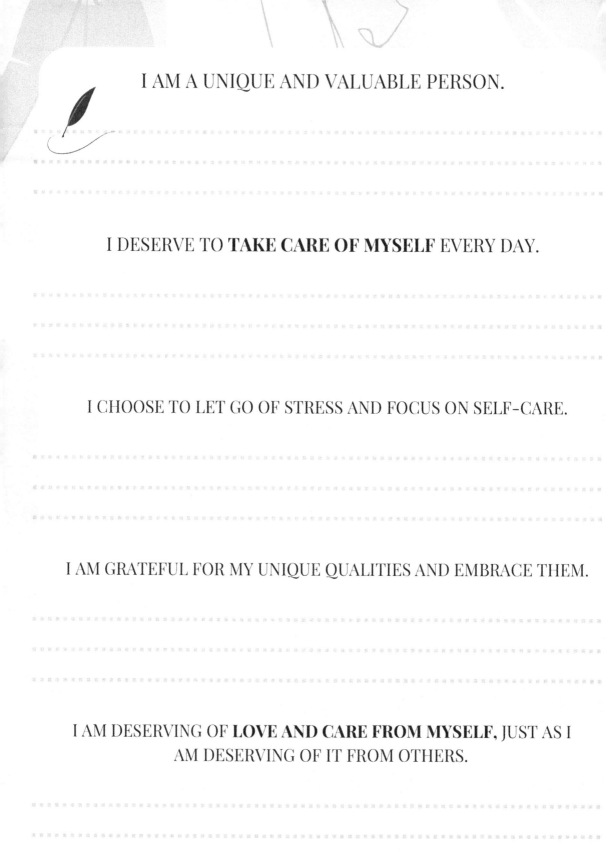

I AM A UNIQUE AND VALUABLE PERSON.

I DESERVE TO **TAKE CARE OF MYSELF** EVERY DAY.

I CHOOSE TO LET GO OF STRESS AND FOCUS ON SELF-CARE.

I AM GRATEFUL FOR MY UNIQUE QUALITIES AND EMBRACE THEM.

I AM DESERVING OF **LOVE AND CARE FROM MYSELF,** JUST AS I
AM DESERVING OF IT FROM OTHERS.

I GIVE MYSELF PERMISSION TO DO WHAT IS RIGHT FOR ME.

I LOVE AND ACCEPT MYSELF FULLY, JUST AS I AM.

I AM PROUD OF WHO I AM AND WHAT I HAVE ACCOMPLISHED,
AND LOOK FORWARD TO WHAT'S TO COME.

I AM ALLOWED TO **PUT MYSELF FIRST**.

I LET GO OF WORRIES THAT DRAIN MY ENERGY.

I ALLOW MYSELF TO **REST AND RECHARGE** WHEN I NEED IT.

I PRIORITIZE MY OWN WELL-BEING AND HAPPINESS EVERY DAY.

PRACTICING SELF-CARE IS THE KINDEST THING I CAN DO
FOR MYSELF AND MY LOVED ONES.

I MAKE TIME FOR HOBBIES AND ACTIVITIES THAT BRING ME JOY.

I RECOGNIZE AND HONOR MY OWN NEEDS AND BOUNDARIES.

I TAKE TIME TO NOURISH MY MIND, BODY, AND SOUL
EVERY DAY.

I CHOOSE TO LET GO OF SELF-CRITICISM AND
EMBRACE SELF-LOVE.

I AM WORTHY OF REST AND RELAXATION.

I TAKE CARE OF MY OWN NEEDS FIRST, KNOWING THAT IT IS
NOT SELFISH, BUT NECESSARY.

MY WELL-BEING IS IMPORTANT AND I MAKE IT A PRIORITY.

I CREATE POSITIVE HABITS THAT SUPPORT MY MIND, BODY, AND SOUL.

EVERY CHOICE I MAKE IS BASED IN SELF-CARE AND SELF-LOVE.

I AM PATIENT AND GENTLE WITH MYSELF AS I NAVIGATE LIFE'S CHALLENGES.

I AM TAKING TIME FOR MYSELF TO RELAX AND UNWIND.

I TAKE CARE OF THE FUTURE BY TAKING CARE OF THE PRESENT MOMENT.

I TAKE TIME TO CELEBRATE MY SUCCESSES AND ACKNOWLEDGE MY PROGRESS.

I EMBRACE MY IMPERFECTIONS AND **LOVE MYSELF UNCONDITIONALLY.**

I RESPECT AND HONOR MYSELF, AND SET BOUNDARIES TO PROTECT MY OWN WELL-BEING.

I LOVE MY IMPERFECT SELF PERFECTLY.

I LISTEN TO MY BODY AND GIVE IT WHAT IT NEEDS.

I AM WORTHY, INSIDE AND OUT.

I MAKE DECISIONS THAT SUPPORT MY HIGHEST GOOD.

I AM OPEN TO SEEKING **HELP AND SUPPORT** WHEN I NEED IT.

I AM GRATEFUL FOR MY UNIQUE QUALITIES AND
APPRECIATE MYSELF FULLY.

I **PRIORITIZE SELF-CARE** AS A VITAL PART OF MY DAILY ROUTINE.

I DESERVE TO FEEL CONFIDENT AND PROUD OF WHO I AM.

I LET GO OF SELF-JUDGMENT AND CRITICISM, AND EMBRACE
SELF-LOVE AND COMPASSION.

I AM MY BIGGEST FAN.

I LOVE THE BODY I WAS BORN WITH.

I AM WORTHY OF TAKING TIME TO PURSUE MY
PASSIONS AND HOBBIES.

I AM MY MAIN FOCUS.

I CHOOSE TO LET GO OF NEGATIVE SELF-TALK AND
REPLACE IT WITH POSITIVITY AND SELF-LOVE.

I LET **MY LOVE FOR MYSELF INCREASE EACH DAY.**

I AM WORTHY OF TAKING TIME FOR MYSELF EACH DAY.

THE MORE I PRACTICE LOVING MYSELF, THE
MORE LOVABLE I BECOME.

I RELEASE THE NEED TO JUDGE MYSELF NEGATIVELY.

I HONOR AND RESPECT MY LIMITATIONS.

THE ONLY APPROVAL I NEED IS MY OWN.

I REWARD MYSELF FOR MY HARD WORK AND DEDICATION.

I AM A GIFT TO THE WORLD.

MY INNER WORLD CREATES MY OUTER WORLD.

I LOVE MYSELF UNCONDITIONALLY BECAUSE I KNOW
THAT **I AM CREATED IN THE IMAGE OF GOD.**

I GIVE MYSELF THE SPACE TO LET GO OF ALL THE
EMOTIONS THAT ARE INSIDE OF ME.

I SURROUND MYSELF WITH THE ENERGY OF LOVE
AND SELF-CARE.

I SAY GOODBYE TO SELF-PITY.

"It's all about falling in love with yourself and sharing that love with someone who appreciates you, rather than looking for love to compensate for a self-love deficit."—Eartha Kitt

"You yourself, as much as anybody in the entire universe, deserve your love and affection."—Buddha

"Self-love is an ocean and your heart is a vessel. Make it full, and any excess will spill over into the lives of the people you hold dear. But you must come first."—Beau Taplin

"A man cannot be comfortable without his own approval."
—Mark Twain

"Talk to yourself like someone you love." – Brené Brown

"DO NOT FEEL LONELY. THE ENTIRE UNIVERSE IS INSIDE YOU. STOP ACTING SO SMALL. YOU ARE THE UNIVERSE IN ECSTATIC MOTION. SET YOUR LIFE ON FIRE."—RUMI

"How you love yourself is how you teach others to love you."
—Rupi Kaur

"THERE IS YOU AND YOU. THIS IS A RELATIONSHIP. THIS IS THE MOST IMPORTANT RELATIONSHIP."—NAYYIRAH WAHEED

"To fall in love with yourself is the first secret to happiness."
—Robert Morely

"You've got to love yourself first. You've got to be okay on your own before you can be okay with somebody else."
— Jennifer Lopez

"I like me. I like my story and all the bumps and bruises. That's what makes me uniquely me."—Michelle Obama

"FRIENDSHIP WITH ONESELF IS ALL-IMPORTANT BECAUSE WITHOUT IT ONE CANNOT BE FRIENDS WITH ANYONE ELSE IN THE WORLD."
—ELEANOR ROOSEVELT

Take a deep breath and turn your focus inward, embracing the importance of self-love and self-care. With each affirmation, feel a growing sense of self-empowerment and kindness towards yourself. By practicing lovingkindness and self-care, you create a solid foundation from which to radiate love and positivity to others.

Conclusion

As our journey with affirmations comes to an end, I want to express my sincere gratitude for choosing to take this journey with me. It has been a true privilege to be a part of your personal growth and self-discovery, and I hope that the affirmations in this book have empowered you to believe in yourself, find fulfillment in your relationships, and live a purposeful and meaningful life.

Remember that at the heart of each affirmation is the powerful concept of gratitude. It has the ability to transform our lives in countless ways, helping us to see the world with new eyes, to appreciate the small things, and to recognize the abundance that surrounds us every day.

Thank you for allowing me to be a part of your journey. It has been an honor and a joy to share this experience with you. And as you continue on your path, may your life be filled with abundance, joy and gratitude. I want you to know how extraordinary and full of power you are. There are unlimited layers of potential within you just waiting to be discovered. Let these words reach your soul and create a spark within you that will ignite the fire of your dreams. Don't be afraid of them. Don't be afraid of success or your own power. You are ready for what life has in store for you. You are ready to take action and get what you want.

Every day when you open your eyes you have the opportunity to begin a new adventure. This is your time. Right now you are ready to take life into your own hands and show the world who you really are. You can walk through life with confidence and self-assurance, knowing that you have everything you need to achieve your goals.

The value you bring to the table is irreplaceable. Your experiences, skills, and passions are unique and worth sharing with the world. Don't let the doubts or opinions of others steal your confidence. You are beautiful in your authenticity and uniqueness.

When you look in the mirror in the morning, tell yourself that you are ready. Ready to take action and participate in the amazing dance of life. See yourself as not only a dreamer but also a doer. This is the key to making your dreams come true - believing that you have the power within you to achieve anything you dream of.

Remember that the process begins with affirmations, but action is more important. Words are powerful, but it is your actions that turn dreams into reality. Allow yourself to experiment, learn from your mistakes, and continually strive to grow. Each step, even the smallest, brings you closer to your dreams.

Dear One, may Daily Whispers with Inspirational Affirmations be your companion in your quest for strength and motivation.
Remember that you deserve to fulfill your dreams and enjoy the beauty that life has to offer. Let your determination become the flame that fuels your actions. Don't be discouraged when you face obstacles, for you have the power within you to overcome them.

Share your accomplishments and successes with other women, for mutual support and inspiration is the key to achieving your dreams. Let your successes inspire others to believe in themselves and follow their desires.

Remember that every day is a new opportunity to get closer to your goal. Trust your instincts and follow your desires, even if the path seems unfamiliar and difficult. Break through your own limitations and discover your unlimited possibilities.

Be brave and don't be afraid to step out of your comfort zone. That's where the greatest discoveries and growth await you. Know that you are capable of surviving and overcoming any adversity. Your determination and perseverance are unquestionable.

I know that you are ready to make this step. The world is waiting for your input, for your voice, and for your dreams to come true.

Step forward with confidence and belief in your abilities. Fulfill your dreams, change the world and inspire others.

YOU ARE EXTRAORDINARY!

YOU ARE BEAUTIFUL!

AND YOU ARE READY FOR WHATEVER LIFE HAS IN STORE FOR YOU!

with LOVE

Amy

Made in the USA
Coppell, TX
03 July 2023